T0327994

# TALKING WITH HANDS

# TALKING WITH HANDS

## EVERYTHING YOU NEED TO START SIGNING NATIVE AMERICAN HAND TALK

A Complete Beginner's Guide with over 200 Words and Phrases

MIKE PAHSETOPAH

# CONTENTS

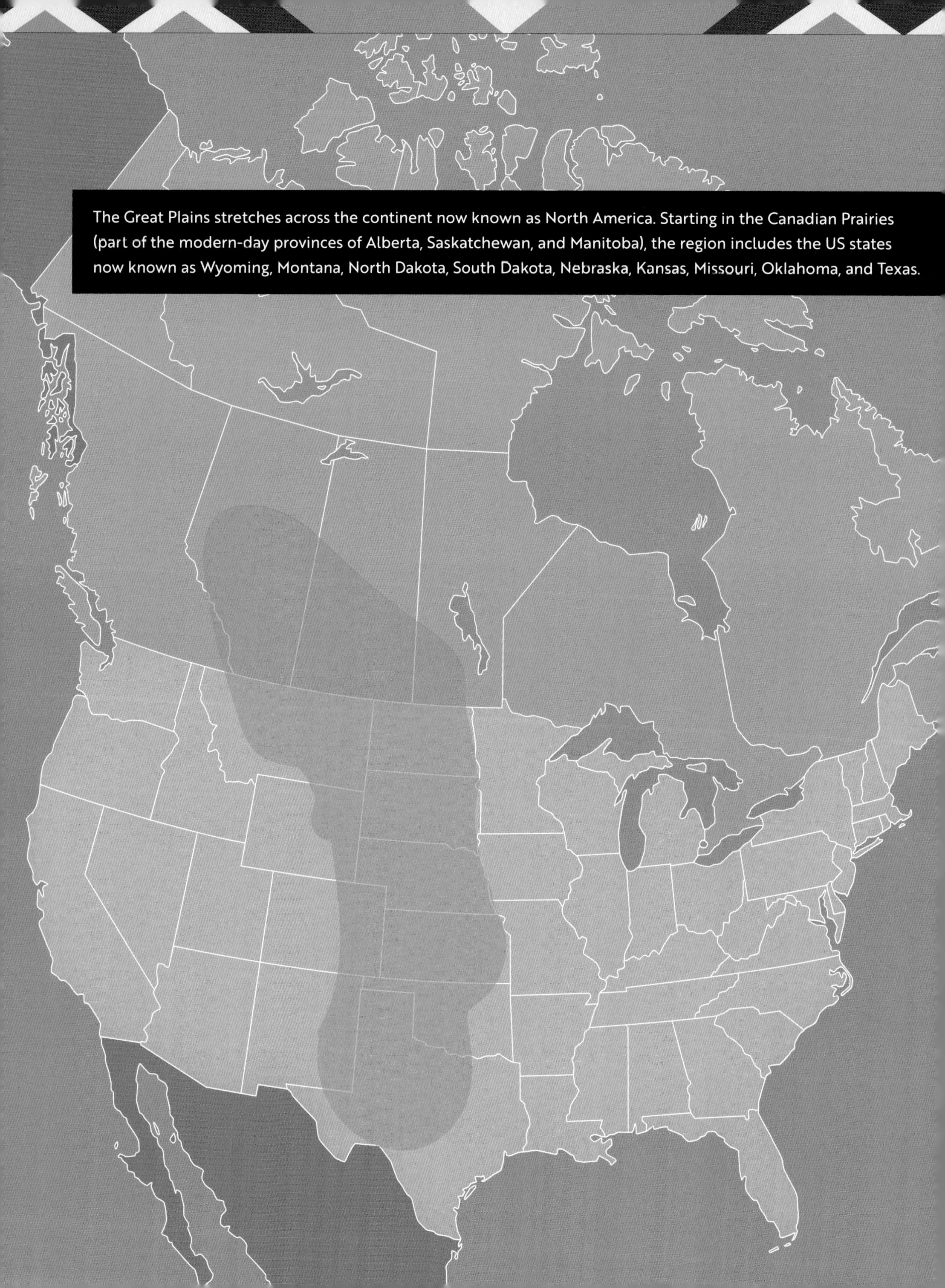
The Great Plains stretches across the continent now known as North America. Starting in the Canadian Prairies (part of the modern-day provinces of Alberta, Saskatchewan, and Manitoba), the region includes the US states now known as Wyoming, Montana, North Dakota, South Dakota, Nebraska, Kansas, Missouri, Oklahoma, and Texas.

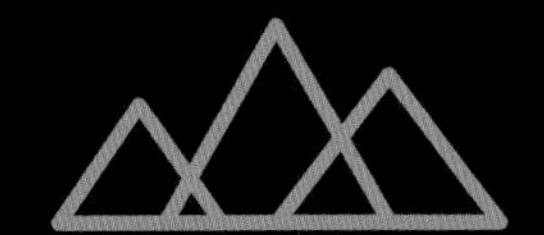

# A BRIEF HISTORY OF HAND TALK

Hand Talk is another term used to describe the numerous Native American sign languages that developed over a period of many centuries, maybe even millennia, among the Indigenous Peoples of North America. And it was called Hand Talk before it was labeled Plains Indian Sign Language (PISL). There are many different tribes in the Great Plains region of the US, including the:

- Aaniiih (also known as the Gros Ventre)
- Arapaho
- Arikara
- Blackfoot
- Cheyenne
- Comanche
- Cree
- Crow
- Dakota
- Hidatsa
- Ho-Chunk
- Kaw
- Kickapoo
- Kiowa
- Lakota
- Mandan
- Nakota
- Nimiipuu
- Ojibwe
- Omaha
- Osage
- Pawnee
- Ponca
- Potawatomie
- Quapaw
- Sac and Fox
- Shoshone
- Tonkawa
- Tsúùtínà
- Ute
- Wichita

One might ask, *Did all tribal nations speak the same Hand Talk?* The answer is no, but there are similarities and differences in the use of Hand Talk across tribes.

So what makes Hand Talk different for each tribe? The culture of each tribe involves different languages, foods, ceremonies, songs, dances, religions, social customs, oral stories and history, as well as family and government structures. After all, not all Natives followed the buffalo and not all lived in tipis. When we look at a map of North America, we see a large land base from Canada extending down through the modern-day states of Wyoming, Montana, North Dakota, South Dakota, Nebraska, Kansas, Missouri, Oklahoma, and Texas. This area that is now known as the Great Plains consisted of many tribal nations who each spoke their own language. It was the spoken linguistic languages that was the backbone of all tribal nations. It was also these languages that separated us. So it was Hand Talk that served as a second primary language among tribes, as a simple means of direct communication. Something to note is that talking with hands, or PISL, was not designed for the deaf and hearing-impaired but as a means of communicating with each other. Still, deaf Native Americans used Hand Talk, too, and it was often their first language. Others who learned the language include frontiersmen and those serving in the military.

An unidentified man, possibly Son of the Star, leader of the Arikara tribe in the late 1800s, demonstrating sign language.

The Plains American Indians were able to communicate in every area and aspect of social life, and thus able to interact together as a people. Tribes would visit with other tribes and were able to commune through hand talking. Hand Talk varied some among tribes, but with the art of hand gestures, facial

Pictures taken of Hastiin To'Haali, a member of the Navajo Nation, at the time he entered the Carlisle Indian Industrial School in Carlisle, Pennsylvania, in 1882 (left) and three years later in 1885 (right). At the school he was given the name Tom Torlino. These (staged) photos were meant to demonstrate the school's mission to "civilize" those of Native American descent, but after leaving the school Hastiin To'Haali returned to his home in New Mexico and resumed his previous lifestyle.

expressions, and body movement, it was easily understood. Talking with hands surpassed the many spoken linguistic languages of Native Americans.

My father used to say, "Our sign language has always been around, son. There is no way of telling how old it really is." I say that today, for as long as Plains Indian Sign Language has existed, talking with hands has also existed. When spoken language was not understood, this form of communication was how we could live together and coexist with other tribal nations. Before Hand Talk was renamed Plains Indian Sign Language, it was used by not only Plains tribes but also by nearly all tribes of the entire US that traveled and interacted with other nations. However, the Hand Talk utilized in the Eastern and Western regions, for example, differed from that used in the Plains region. It is this same sign language from the Plains region that is one of the most well documented, most likely because of its high number of speakers, said to be in the tens of thousands up until the late nineteenth century. Maybe that was because the more nomadic lifestyles of the numerous Plains tribes meant more contact with neighboring tribes, and so more need and opportunity to communicate in sign language.

## THE MAN-MADE DECLINE OF HAND TALK

Eventually Hand Talk became almost completely broken and lost, and the explanation is sad and heartbreaking. The language declined to the point where the number of speakers went from being in the tens of thousands (as mentioned above) to only about a few dozen fluent hand talkers today. The truth is this was not a natural decline. During the time of westward expansion, the US government thought that if

Grey Whirlwind communicating in sign language with writer Ernest Thompson Seton, July 1927.

it could destroy Native American culture, that would aid in the destruction of tribal nations, promoting a unified "American" culture. The government built boarding schools in which to place Native babies and children in an attempt to wipe out Native culture and language by banning its speech and practice in these institutions. The schools were designed to convert children to a colonial system of life, and they were punished severely if they ever expressed any part of the culture into which they had been born and grown up. They could not wear their traditional clothes nor display any other aspects of their culture in their appearance. They were forced to abandon their birth names that had been given to them with consideration and care and adopt English names instead. A lot of abuse and deaths occurred in these institutions, and when the surviving kids came out of the system, many did not know their own culture or language, nor could they speak with their hands, as they were forbidden to do so. Native deaf speakers were taught American Sign Language (ASL) instead, despite the fact that ASL was in part influenced by the Northeast variant of Native American sign language. Because the languages were being actively suppressed, consequently there could be no new generation of speakers who would then pass down their language to their descendants. At the beginning of this paragraph, I mentioned the words "broken" and "lost." I mean "broken" in the sense that Hand Talk is not spoken or signed as fluently as it was in the past, and thus was nearly "lost."

## A RACE AGAINST TIME

However, there were (and are) still some tribes or individuals who kept Hand Talk alive, because it was an important means of communication for them. In September 1930, Hugh L. Scott, a US Army general who had learned Hand Talk during his career based in the American West, organized a gathering called the Indian Sign Language Grand Council, hosted by the Blackfoot Nation of Montana. This council brought together eighteen participants representing a dozen Native American tribes and language groups. Their proceedings were filmed, the largest such gathering of Indigenous leaders ever captured on camera. The group sought to document and preserve Hand Talk for future generations. At the beginning of the video, Scott expresses his concern that the language will soon be lost due to its lack of speakers. This video was part of $5,000 in federal funding Scott had secured for language preservation efforts, but external factors such as the Great Depression and Scott's own death in 1934 hindered further development. The footage itself, which was stowed away in the depths of the National Archives, was only rediscovered in the early twenty-first century, in line with current language preservation efforts.

## HAND TALK FOR THE PRESENT AND FUTURE

Today, Hand Talk is slowly being rediscovered and revitalized. Language camps, open to those of Native or non-Native descent of all ages, aim to teach the basics of the language in a way that rings true to how Indigenous languages are best taught. Speakers also instruct the language through workshops or demonstrations at schools and colleges. For example, as a cultural educator I regularly present aspects of Native culture, including Hand Talk, at public schools and universities. Another important development is advocating for the language to be incorporated into a school's curriculum. As long as people continue to learn Hand Talk and work together to preserve the language, it will never entirely go away.

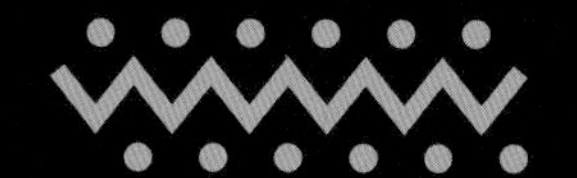

# PERSONAL REFLECTIONS ON HAND TALK

Now, allow me to formally introduce myself. My name is Michael Pahsetopah. I am Osage and Cherokee on my father's side and Muscogee Creek and Yuchi on my mother's side. I am a champion fancy dancer and Native Hand Talk performer, entertainer, educator, storyteller, artist, craftsman, flutist, and speaker. I have traveled throughout the US and presented to a vast array of audiences demonstrating Native storytelling, song, and dance at many schools, libraries, and colleges. I am very grounded in my culture, and that makes it really easy to share all the teachings I have learned from my father. My profession is a way of teaching and preserving culture, beliefs, and languages. I think it is important to learn and share more about my cultural heritage and how Hand Talk is a normal part of life for me. It's always important to learn all aspects of Native culture, such as how we think, talk, and view life, and it's crucial in order to get a full understanding of how Hand Talk is learned and used.

OPPOSITE: The author signing the word *speak* (page 98)

It is also important to note that oral history is a part of Native culture and that this book contains information that has been passed down or learned from family and friends. So there will be few works cited or references. Instead, much of it is knowledge gained from my teachings and my ancestors.

## FAMILY HISTORY WITH HAND TALK



I am a fourth-generation hand talker. Family history has been passed down to my father from my grandfathers. I was a young boy when I was exposed and introduced to Hand Talk. (Looking back, Dad was good at keeping my great-grandfather's memory alive. He told the same stories throughout my life and they became a part of my DNA.) I have extensive knowledge in the rich cultural heritage and history of my father and grandfathers. So you could say I have the highest level of education in Native American culture. Hand Talk is a part of that culture because that is how my family conversed, along with spoken language. We would either speak English and use Hand Talk at the same time, or, with my Osage relatives, we would speak Osage and Hand Talk at the same time.

Let me share the legacy of how talking with hands became a part of me. It goes back to my great-grandfather, who lived from 1870 to 1938. He was a full-blooded Osage and was of the Buffalo Bull clan. At the age of three, he and his family walked from Kansas to Oklahoma with a band of Osage people, crossing over the Neosho River. After finally reaching their destination, they resided in Pawhuska, Oklahoma. My great-grandfather's name was Pahsetopah Shompanashe (called Pi by the family). Interpreted, *Shompanashe* refers to "four Buffalo Bulls in the distance, standing dark like a silhouette." *Pahsetopah* literally means "four Buffalo Bulls at a vertical, at a distance, where you see the humps on their backs, seeing 'four hills.'" As an explanation, it would mean as if you are looking at four buffalo from a distance that are in a straight line, but because they are so far away from you, they almost look like four hills due to the humps on their backs.

At the age of twelve, Pi was in a horse race and his horse toppled over on top of him. His injuries from that accident were permanent and left him deaf. The world as he knew it became silenced. Soon after, he learned Hand Talk from a Ponca man with the last name of Williams, and that's how he came to know about it.

When he was twenty years old, Pi jumped on his horse and headed for South Dakota. He became friends with a Lakota man named

Whirlwind Soldier, whose family later adopted him and considered Pi like a brother. He lived there for about ten years, then came back home to his Osage people. He met my traditional, full-blooded Osage great-grandmother, Veva Spencer, of the Deer clan from Hominy, Oklahoma. She spoke fluent Osage and learned how to talk with her hands from Pi. They had five children together and they all spoke fluent Osage and talked with their hands. She passed away at the age of thirty-eight, and Pi raised the children.

Pi was a prominent figure in the town of Pawhuska. He led parades riding his favorite horse, wearing his full-length eagle-feather war bonnet, and playing his flute—a photograph survives where he is riding behind First Lady Eleanor Roosevelt in a parade in Pawhuska. He then rode his horse from Pawhuska to Washington, DC, in order to lead the Oklahoma delegation in a presidential parade.

My great-grandpa Pi was a fantastic entertainer and showman even though he was deaf and spoke with talking hands. He was known to be a storyteller and people said his fingers moved very fast in motion, in addition to his use of pantomime and gestures. His sign language was easy to understand by anyone, even non-Natives. In 1938, at the age of sixty-eight, Pi passed away, when my grandpa, Chris Pahsetopah (Pappa), was just twenty-five years old and my dad was six. Pappa kept his father's story alive for my dad, Paul Pahsetopah, and then to me, through Hand Talk and oral history.

As a little boy, I was very shy and bashful, but I could talk with my hands and it was said I would grow up to be like Pi. I remember when I was in the first grade, my teacher asked me to stand up and say my name. She told me to stand up straight and take my hands out of my pockets. I kept my hands in my pockets to keep from using Hand Talk. I whispered to her that I didn't want to because I talked with my hands and that the kids would make fun of me. She said, "Do what would make you comfortable." I said, "I like to dance." She asked me if I would like to dance for the class and I eagerly said, "Yes!" After she introduced me, all the kids made a circle around me and I danced.

That same year my Pappa suffered an injury to his throat and was unable to speak for a long period of time. I would go visit him while he was in the hospital and as the healthcare workers did not understand Hand Talk, they taught him to spell in American Sign Language. When he returned home from the hospital, he combined Hand Talk and ASL. Soon, his voice returned and he would get tickled at my use of Hand Talk. He would say, "Yeah, that's good," or "When are you going to dance again? Want to come watch you." He used his raspy, low-sounding voice and mixed Hand Talk and ASL as he conversed for the rest of his life.

My dad was a good teacher to me, and Hand Talk became a natural part of our communication. Today, I view it as my responsibility to teach and share this Hand Talk with this generation and those that will follow.



## RECOGNIZING THE IMPORTANCE OF HAND TALK AND SPOKEN LANGUAGES

Sometimes, someone will ask: "Why do you talk with your hands?" or "Why do you dance wearing those feathers?"

The simple answer is culture. In Oklahoma, there are thirty-seven federal sovereign tribal nations. Many realized that they were losing their language and so they began looking for those who could speak fluently to revitalize spoken language through language programs. During that time, Hand Talk was nearly a dead language here in Oklahoma. "Broken" is a good way to describe it, as I have mentioned earlier.

In the mid-1970s, I began to notice a decline in Hand Talk. By the 1980s, it was hard to use because no one communicated that way except a few ole-timers. At home, my father continued talking with his hands. He used Hand Talk daily, mixed in with his English words, and he would often make hand motions, bodily movements, and facial expressions to accompany the signs he used. He was very animated and even my friends understood what he was saying. For the most part, however, only a few would use simple signs like "good," "food," "water," "go," and "yes." Those were the simple signs that I would say over the last twenty years because those were the only signs people would use.

Nowadays, there is a new movement where non-Native society is recognizing how Native culture was almost destroyed and how important everyone's cultures are to the wider society. Tribes are establishing language programs in schools and at home. This book is a huge step in bringing Hand Talk back to the forefront of revitalizing what was almost lost. Language is such an important part of culture, and part of preserving cultural heritage lies in preserving the language.

## UNDERSTANDING THE BASICS

Plains Indian Sign Language is visual, so you must watch and observe things. But you may also need to listen sometimes, because speakers may choose to combine Hand Talk with a spoken language that they use. When we see and think, we add signing because everything begins with a thought. You must remember PISL was intended as communication between tribal nations with different languages. As a result, Hand Talk is simple and direct. In English, to say that the weather is hot, you might say something like, "It's hot outside." In Hand Talk, the signs you would use to express the same idea would directly translate into English as something like "hot out."

Regarding my Hand Talk, let it be known that I'm only teaching my way. And it's not the only way, because in life we have many teachers.

### The Basics

When teaching, I always begin with the simple basics and build on skills as your knowledge increases. For example, a sign needs what I call a "descriptor," which I define as a simple mechanical animation. And by that I mean a gesture, a facial expression, pantomime, and/or body movement. There is no rule that says you can't use descriptors because I feel that these expressions make it easier for people who don't know Hand Talk to understand what someone is signing.

When I'm talking with my hands, I quickly consider my audience and how I can be sensitive with my teaching. The first question I usually get is: Which hand do I start with?

The right hand is the dominant hand used in Hand Talk, whether or not you are right-hand dominant. The right hand shows the action—whether it is in the past, present, or future. In signing, the right hand also shows the subject, noun, and verb. The left hand is used to convey more complex ideas or phrases. These are the simple fundamentals of Hand Talk.

In this book, we will start off with simple signs that we can use with the index finger of the right hand. There are many that we will learn. Then we will incorporate the usage of the left hand to form more signs. Thus, you will learn many of the signs in Hand Talk.

One thing to remember is that there is no formal alphabet in Hand Talk, nor are there names for days of the week or months of the year. Instead, for example, we use words like "winters" or "moons" to measure seasons and years.

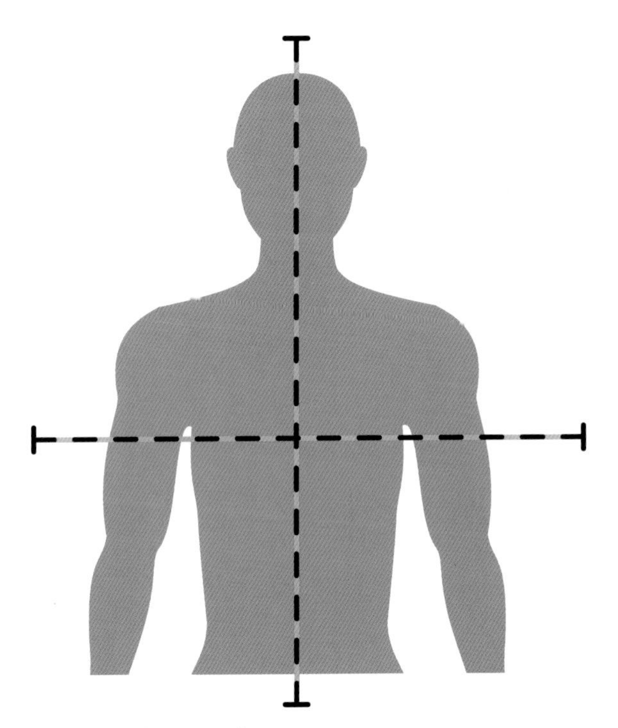

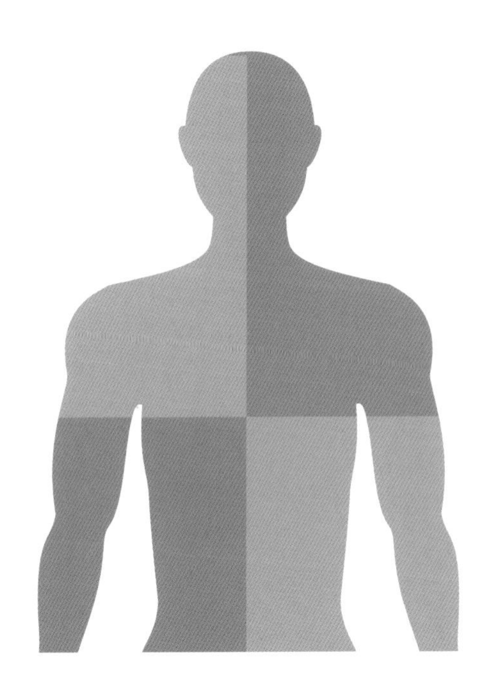

## Centerline Theory

Centerline theory is designed for hand positioning. This is really important because there are so many similarities in these signs. I always want to make sure that learners' hands are in the right place. When you're practicing, imagine that a line runs from the top of your head down the center of your body and another runs horizontally right across your heart. Imagine the four quadrants formed by these lines: top right, top left, bottom right, and bottom left.

Whether your hands are to the left or right of the vertical line, or above or below the horizontal line, all these considerations matter to convey the meaning of your signs. For example, the signs for *father* and *mother* (see pages 78 and 79) both involve placing your right hand on your chest, but whether you place it to the right or the left of the vertical centerline makes a difference. Centerline theory also may involve leaning left or right, away from the centerline, because to me that adds feeling—these gestures help make what you're doing more understandable. There may be signs that we use that are waist down (for example, *flood* and *child* on pages 63 and 79, respectively) and signs that are very similar but differ because they are positioned against quadrants or the centerline (for example, *done* on page 161).

Centerline theory helps you remember where your audience is and how they see the signs you're making. While I can teach big groups of people how to make signs, hand talking is really about direct communication between people.

## A NOTE ON THE TITLE

This book comes from both what I've learned from my father and from my documented personal notes, drawings, and lessons. Over time, these lessons became a curriculum program that I called "Talking with Hands." As I have stated, Native American sign language was first called Hand Talk. Then it was labeled "Plains Indian Sign Language." And I myself renamed it Talking with Hands. This was because many of my students were American Indian, but were not members of tribes associated with the Plains region. I didn't want to exclude or limit anyone wanting to learn.

## HOW TO USE THIS BOOK

In this book, the English translation of the sign will be at the top of the photo diagram, and any directions or notes will follow underneath. Cultural notes will also be provided throughout to provide context for certain words or phrases.

Our American Indian language and Hand Talk were never meant to be interpreted by English speakers. The English language is very limited when trying to convey how a word of a Native language is meant to be interpreted, due to linguistic differences among Native languages. Regarding the signs included in this book, I have done my best to equate them with what would be their English equivalents.

Hand Talk is still the purest form of direct communication, so always keep in mind to be loose and relaxed, including in your shoulders. I would suggest some type of finger and hand stretches just so your hands don't tense up. If your hands are tense, it can be very easy to make an incorrect sign.

Lastly, feel free to implement any facial expression, whether it is a smile or something else that shows you are serious, sad, or excited, because that is an important part of this communication style.

Thank you for joining me and I hope to meet you down the road of Hand Talk.

# BASICS USING ONE FINGER

OPPOSITE: The author signing the word *up* (page 22)

## I/ME

Point your right thumb at your chest.

## YOU

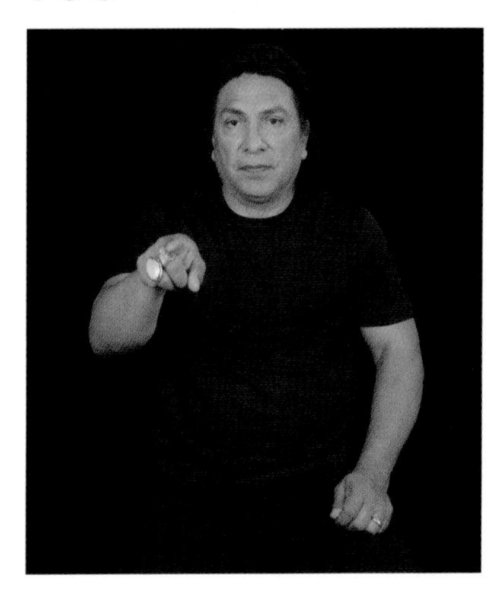

The index finger should be pointed away from yourself, slightly askew/not straight on.

---

*We never directly point at a person but instead in their general direction. Back in the old days, ours was a warrior society, so while pointing directly at a person is not so much insulting, avoiding it can keep you out of trouble. No one can misinterpret you pointing at them and respond, "Oh, you want some of me?!" Be kind and polite and point in their direction but not right at them.*

## UP

Place the right index finger at head level.

---

*While you may move your finger slightly upward, don't extend your arm above your head. That's another sign.*

## DOWN

With your right arm extended slightly to the side of the body, your right index finger points down.

## ARISE

Begin with the right index finger pointing away from you, palm up. Bend your arm at the elbow while keeping the index finger extended.

## STAND

This sign is performed very similarly to *up*, but start your right index finger at a lower position and move it up deliberately and slowly.

---

*Hand positioning when talking with hands is key. Many signs are very similar to each other, and the same sign done in a different place (higher, lower, or to the right or left side of the centerline) may mean something else. Take* stand, *for example; if you begin the sign higher, it could be mistaken for* up.

## COME

Fully extend your right finger from your chest, then draw it slowly toward you.

## GO

With your right palm open on your chest, swing your arm away from you, almost as if you're shooing something away.

---

*Some signs look similar to each other, but depending on the mood or emotion you convey when you're making them, their meaning will change.*

## RUN

The right index finger begins over the right shoulder and casts forward, almost like you're casting a fishing rod.

## ALONE

Your right index finger starts at the throat at the centerline, then the index finger glides outward, tracing a dip down and swirl up at the end.

*In* alone, *the finger does a little dip down and swoop up at the end of the motion.*

## BRING

Point to what you would like to bring with your right pointer finger, then move your pointer finger toward your chest.

*Some hand talkers will say* bring *starting with an open hand, then grasp and pull their hand toward the body, almost like they're grabbing something to bring toward them.*

## TRUTH

Your right index finger starts at the chest. Extend this finger straight out.

*Make sure your finger moves in a straight line away from your chest. It means that whatever you're saying, the words are straight.*

## LIGHTNING

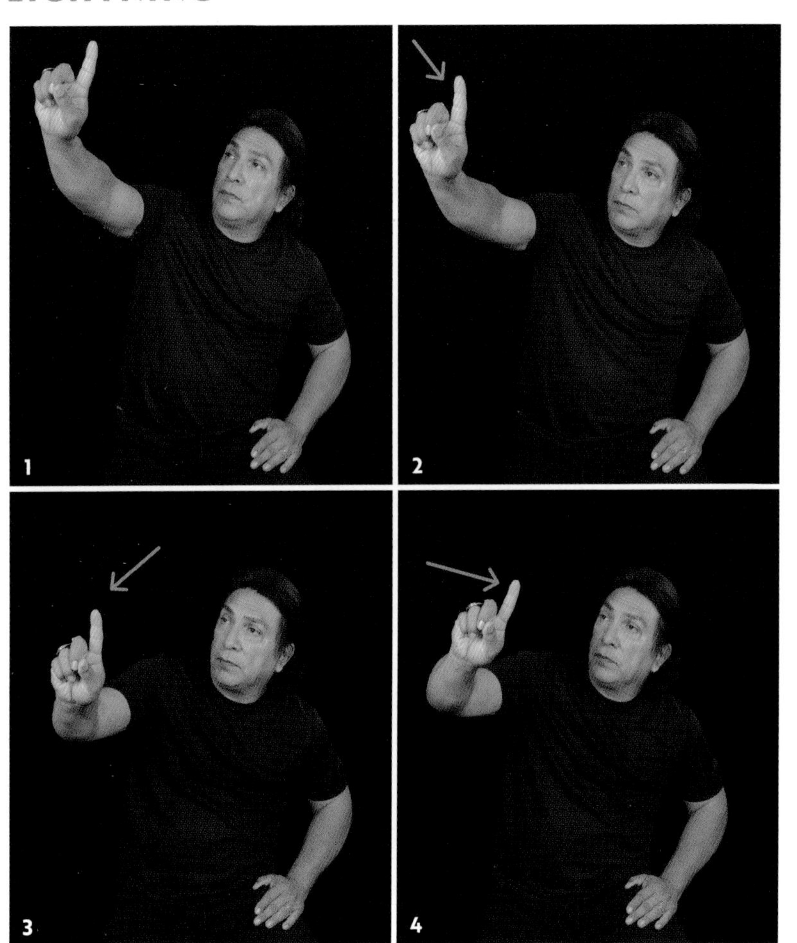


Extend the right finger away from your chest and make a zigzag motion, like a bolt of lightning.

## NOW

With the right index finger at the centerline, point down, then emphasize it by pointing down three times, almost like you're pointing to the present moment.

---

*Centerline theory (page 18) helps us differentiate* down *from* now, *which is a similar sign but done at different orientations to the centerline.* Down *is done to the right of the centerline, whereas* now *is signed right at the centerline.*

## CIRCLE

With your index finger, point up and draw a circle. Draw this circle away from and toward the body, rather than vertically to the viewer.

---

*The sign for* circle *depends on the type of circle we mean. The shape uses the pointer finger. If we mean a council meeting (see page 154) of people gathered, sitting in a circle, we use our fists. If we mean to circle around something, we circle our right index finger around our extended left-hand fingers. To circle around a tree, we circle our right index finger around our extended left index finger.*

## SNAKE

LEFT: Beginning with your right index finger pulled toward the side of your body, palm face down, squiggle the finger outward from your body, as if tracing the shape of a snake.

BELOW: Shake your finger to indicate a rattlesnake's rattle.

## RATTLESNAKE

# COUNTING UP TO ONE HUNDRED

OPPOSITE: The author signing the word ***one*** (page 30)

### ONE

### TWO

### THREE

### FOUR

### FIVE

### SIX

## SEVEN

## EIGHT

## NINE

## TEN

## ELEVEN

Tap your open left palm with your right hand to represent *ten*, then hold up your right pinky finger to show *eleven*.

## TWENTY

## THIRTY

## FORTY

## FIFTY

## ONE HUNDRED

When we go into tens, we close our left palm into a fist, then grasp the left pinky with our right hand to represent *ten*, ring finger to represent *twenty*, middle finger to represent *thirty*, index finger to represent *forty*, and thumb to represent *fifty*.

To represent numbers beyond *fifty*, close the left palm into a fist again, then grasp the left pinky again, this time to represent *sixty*, the ring finger to represent *seventy*, the middle finger to represent *eighty*, the index finger to represent *ninety*, and then the thumb to represent *one hundred*. Show the open right palm.

Another school of Hand Talk shows *one hundred* with both palms open, facing the viewer, while the right hand waves.

## TWENTY-FIVE

After using both hands to represent ten, show "two tens" by extending the pinky and ring fingers of your left hand. Then count to five by pointing to each of the five fingers of your right hand.

## SEVENTY-EIGHT

Go through the usual process of counting the tens to show *seventy*, then show *eight*.

---

*Hand Talk is supposed to be real simple and basic, nothing complicated. Yet it gets complicated when we try to explain it using English.*

# TIME & TENSES

OPPOSITE: The author signing the word *present* (page 36)

**When we are talking about time, remember the action always happens with the right hand.**

## PRESENT

## PAST

Extend the right and left index fingers side by side, as you do for *present*. Then the right index finger moves backward "in time."

*When signing tenses, be sure to move your finger in a straight line. Moving your right finger out and to the side is a different sign.* *(See* around *on page 91.)*

## FUTURE

Extend the right and left index fingers side by side, as you do for *present*. Then, the right index finger moves forward "in time."



## LONG TIME PAST

The right index finger moves farther back, as if it's moving far back in time.

## FAR IN THE FUTURE

The right index finger moves farther forward, as if it's moving far forward in time.

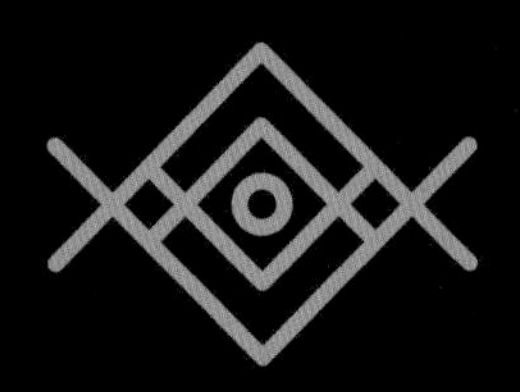

# CELESTIAL BODIES

OPPOSITE: The author signing the word *stars* (page 40)

## SUN

Form a circle with the thumb and index finger of your right hand. Your other fingers should gently curve as well.

## STARS

Flick the fingers of both hands above your head, as if you're flicking water into the sky, rotating your body slightly as you do. Turn your face and eyes upward as you perform this action.

## SUN IS HOT

First, sign the word for *sun,* then show the rays beating down by pointing the fingers of your right hand toward your head. In English, this sign would translate to "The sun is hot."

## MOON

**The sun would always symbolize a day, but because of the way Native people observed the moon, whenever they would begin to measure time beyond a day, they would go by the moon. The sun is going to stay in the same place, but counting new moons would help determine the seasons.**

## FULL MOON

This idea also translates into English as "The moon is full."

## NO MOON

## YOU SEE MOON?

This phrase uses four signs in succession: the question indicator sign (page 144), *you* (page 22), *see* (page 106), and *moon* (page 41). In English, it would translate to "Do you see the moon?"

*I cover questions on page 143, but in this example, you can see that we don't use the word* do *to start questions like these.*

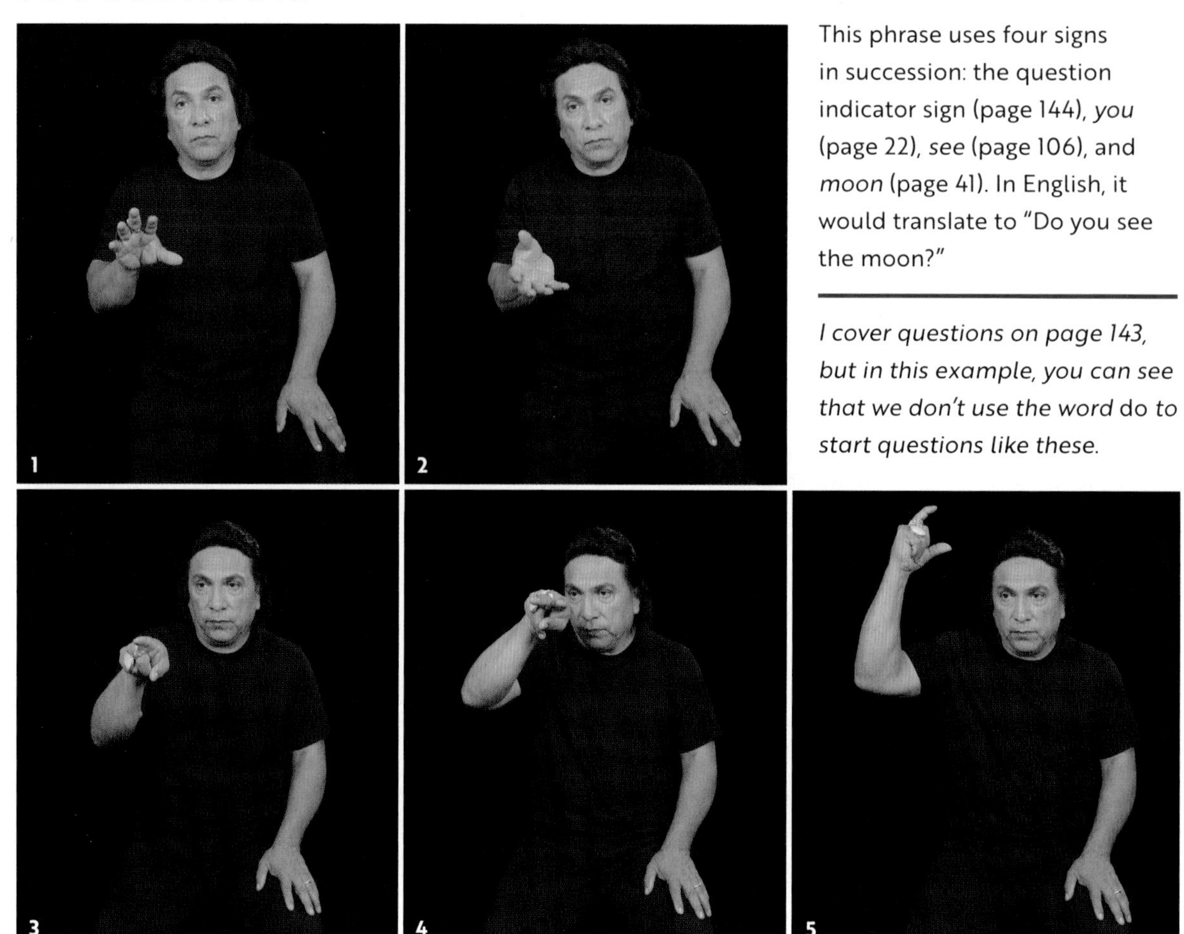

## FULL MOON TONIGHT

This phrase would translate to English as "The moon is full tonight."

# TIME OF DAY

OPPOSITE: The author signing the word *noon* (page 46)

## MORNING

Here, you need to face the east and sign the word *sun* (page 40) toward that direction.

## NOON

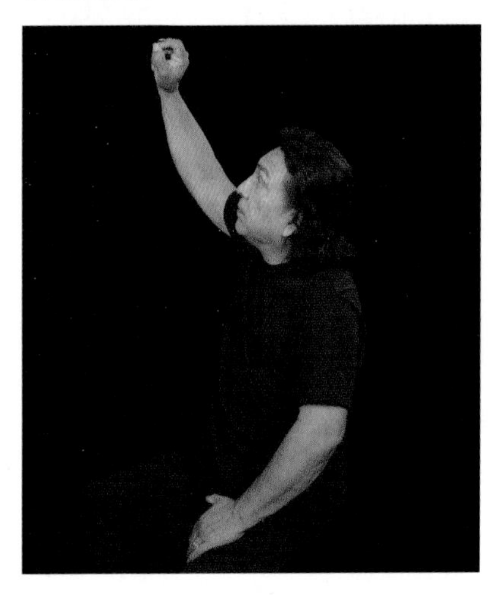

Sign the word for *sun* straight above your head, at the centerline.

## AFTERNOON

Drop your hand a bit down from noon, like the sun moving lower in the sky.

## EVENING

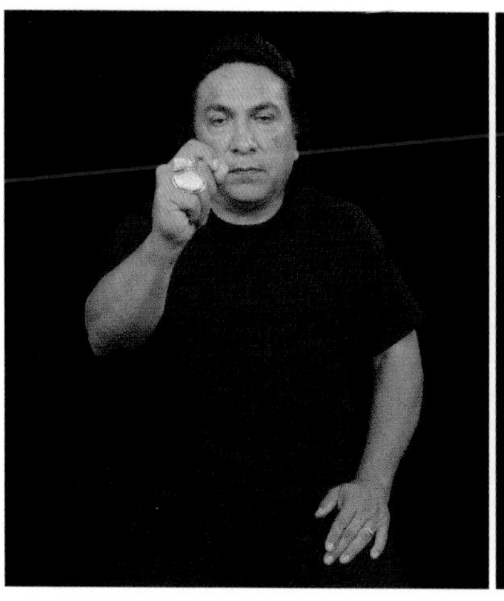

The sun drops down from *afternoon*. Follow up with the sign for *night*.

## DAY

## NIGHT

Join your hands above your head in a rainbow shape, with your right hand over your left.

---

*This symbol is kind of like closure—the closure of the day.*

*Some Natives will do the sign for* night *closer to their forehead or farther above their heads. There's so much diversity between cultures from tribe to tribe. Whenever I talk with other hand talkers, we sign with each other and observe what's different. Instead of correcting each other, we add more of each other's signs to our own vocabulary.*

## GOOD MORNING

Rather than signing *good* first in *good morning*, we start with the symbol for *morning*.



## COLD EVENING

For the word *cold*, place your two fists at collarbone level and move your body in a slight shiver, as if you are miming pulling a blanket up around your body.

## I GO AFTERNOON

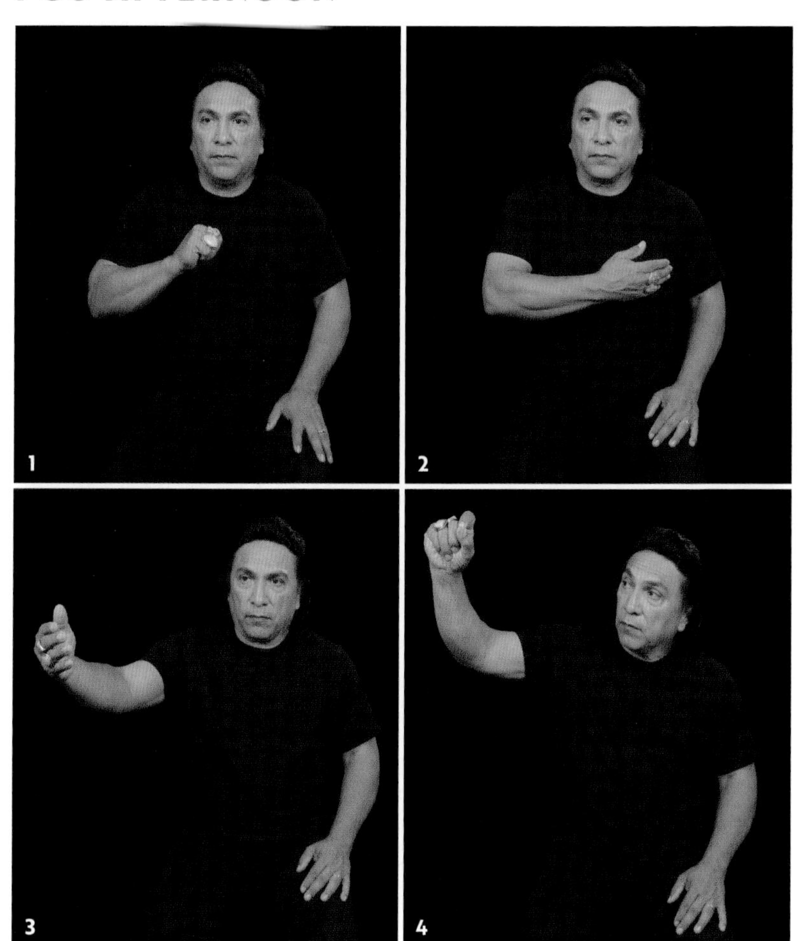


For this phrase, sign these three signs in succession: *I* (page 22), *go* (page 24), and *afternoon* (page 46). In English this phrase would translate to "I'm going this afternoon."

# SEASONS

OPPOSITE: The author signing the word *moon* (page 41)

To indicate seasons, we begin every sequence of signs with the sign for the moon.

## SUMMER

To express the word for *summer*, sign these three words in succession: *moon* (page 41), *sun* (page 40), and *hot* (page 40). You can also use the sign for *summer* to express the idea that "summer is hot" (translated literally as "summer hot").

## FALL

Mimic the leaves falling with your fingers.

## WINTER

It's important to emphasize that the hands are shivering in the sign for *winter*, moving back and forth three times.

## SPRING

This word combines the signs for the words *moon* (page 41) and *grow* (page 97).

## COLD

## HEAT

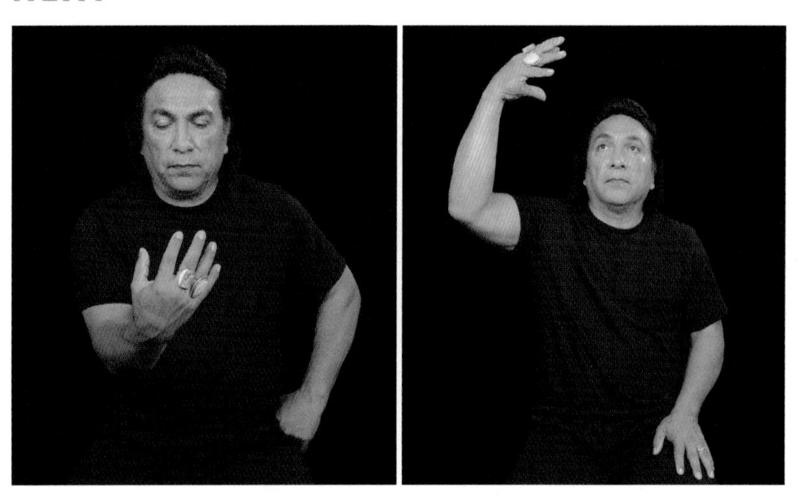

The sign for *heat* incorporates the sign for *hot* (page 40).

## LEAVES FALL FROM THE TREE

## WINTER'S COMING

This phrase combines the signs for the words *come* (page 24), *moon* (page 41), and *cold* (page 53).

## GRASS COMING UP OUT OF THE EARTH

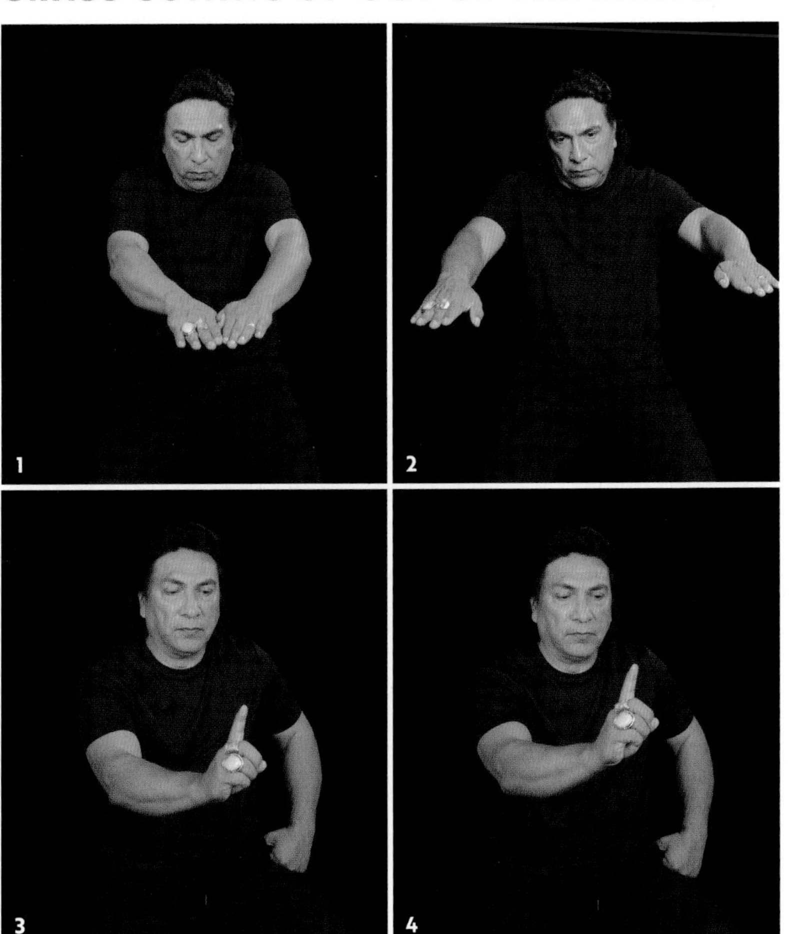


This word combines the signs for the words *earth (page 72)* and *grow (page 97)*.

**It's been a custom among many Plains American Indians to be more descriptive and intricate regarding the seasons. Some would make the sign for the moon before each season. There was a belief that the moon brought the seasons. My ancestors were very observant regarding nature, which you can see in the words for *fall* (page 52), *winter* (page 53), *spring* (page 53), and *summer* (page 52).**

# YEARS & AGE

OPPOSITE: The author asking, "How many winters are you?" (page 58)

**Years were measured in winters—and the sign for one winter equals one year. So to tell someone how old you are, you would do the sign for winter, then do the counting signs until you reach how many winters you've been through. I'm sixty-four winters.**

## HOW MANY WINTERS ARE YOU?

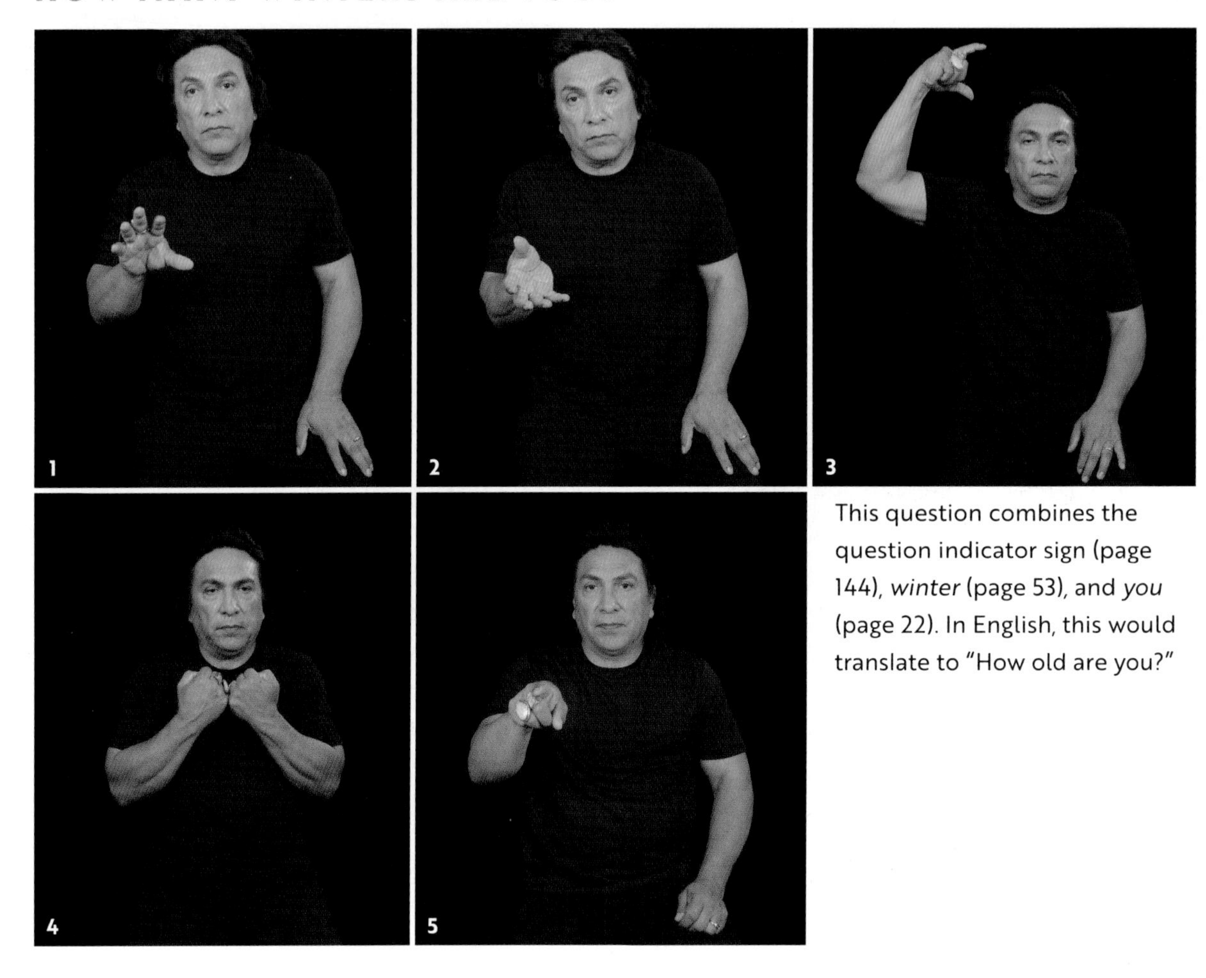


This question combines the question indicator sign (page 144), *winter* (page 53), and *you* (page 22). In English, this would translate to "How old are you?"

## I MOVED FIVE WINTERS AGO . . .

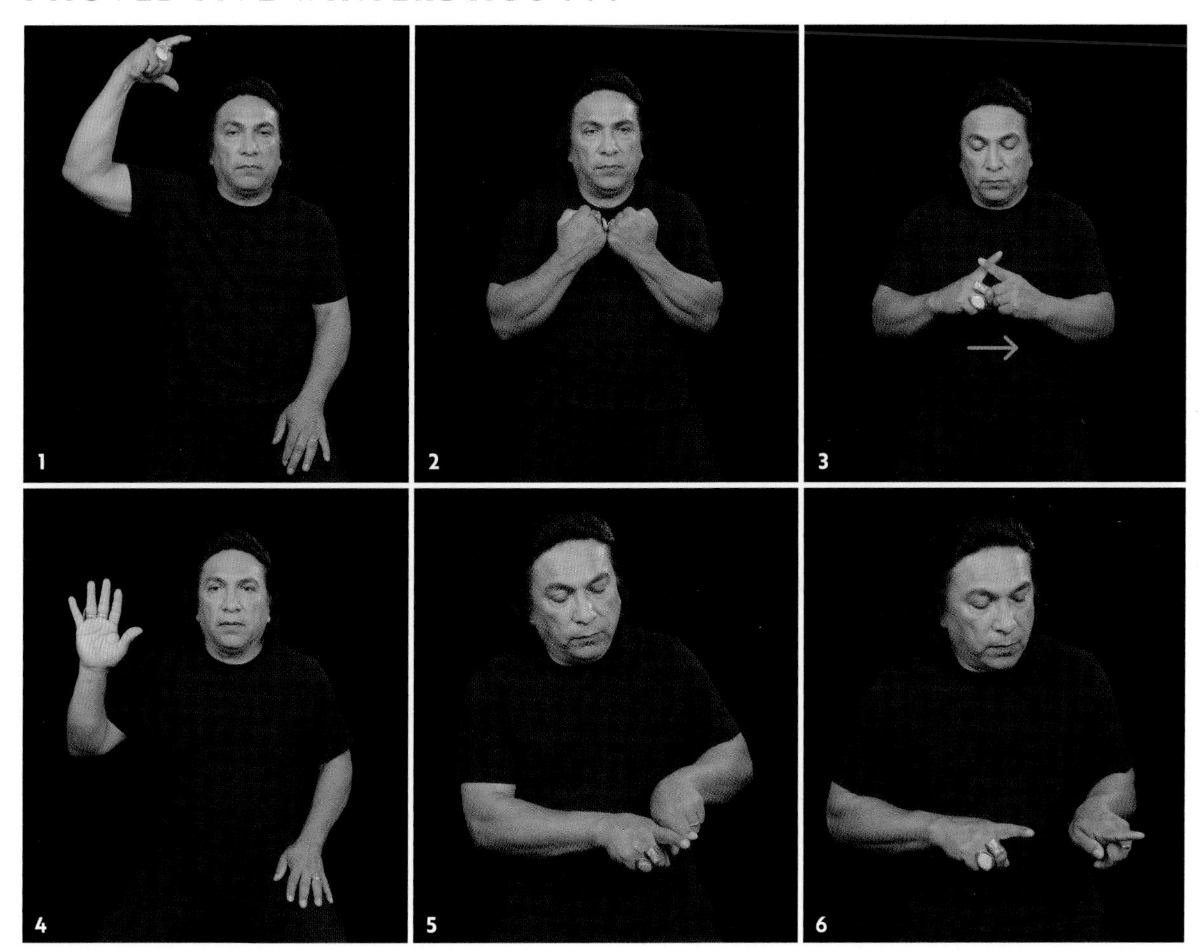


To say *move*, use your right and left index fingers to create a tipi shape and move your fingers to the right. This phrase combines the words for *winter* (page 53), *move*, *five* (page 30), and *past* (pag 36).

# WEATHER

OPPOSITE: The author signing the word *rain* (page 62)

## WIND

Start with both of your hands palms down in front of you and to the left. Shimmy your hands as you pull them back to your right.

---

*Both hands should quiver.*

## RAIN

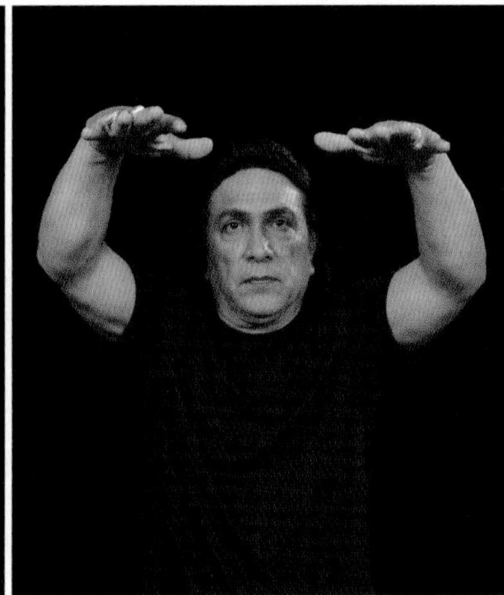

## TORNADO

With your right index finger held up and to the side, spiral it downward in a funnel shape.

## SNOW

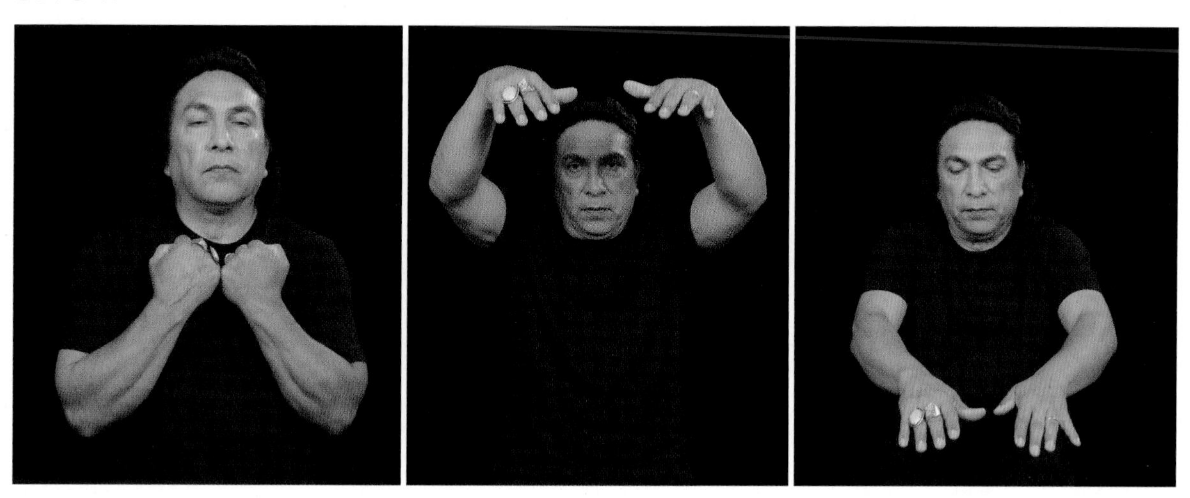

To express the word for *snow*, sign the word for *cold* (page 53) and then drop your hands in a falling motion.

---

*The "falling down" element of the sign for* snow *looks similar to the sign for* fall, *with the leaves falling down. That's why it's important to show the first step of each sign to differentiate it.* Snow *begins with the sign for* cold, *while* fall *begins with* tree *(page 73).*

## FLOOD

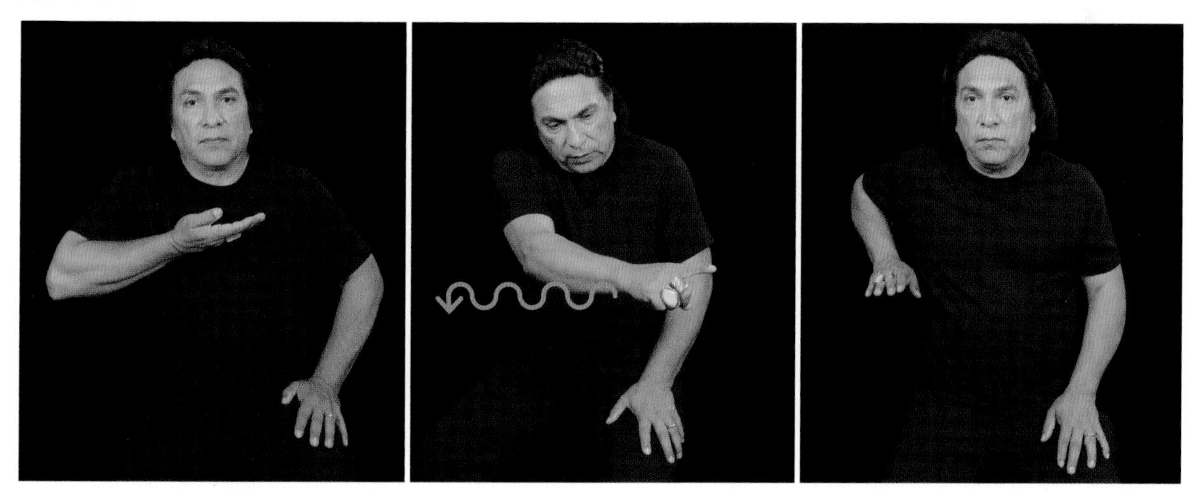

Place your right hand, palm side up, at chest level to indicate *water*. Then, sign the word *river* by pointing your right index finger to the left and slowly trace a gently swooping line horizontally across your chest (see page 72 for more details). Afterward, show the water level of the flood by indicating its height relative to your body.

---

*The flood could be waist high, chest level, or above your head . . .*

# ANIMALS

OPPOSITE: The author signing the word *deer* (page 67)

## BIRD

Flap your palms up and down, like a bird.

## EAGLE

The difference between the bird and the eagle is that the eagle's wings are outstretched and it glides, which you can illustrate with a tilt to the body.

## BEAR

Pull your fingers back on both palms and position them like a bear's ears atop your head.

## DEER

Stretch out the fingers on both of your hands and position them like antlers atop your head. Move your fingers outward slightly.

## ELK

*Elk* is very close to *deer*, but the antlers are bigger, shown by your hands being farther from your head.

## BEAVER

Flap your right hand up and down, like the paddle of a beaver's tail.

## FISH

Hold your right hand slightly in front of you, with your thumb pointing upward. Mime swimming like a fish by waving your palm left and right.

## TURTLE

Form a fist with your right hand, then move your right hand slowly forward to indicate a turtle's slow movements.

---

*Before moving your right hand shaped into a fist, you can tap the top of it with your left hand to indicate that the shell is hard.*

## CAT

Push your nose up with your right index finger.

*If you're indicating a big cat—like a mountain lion—do the sign for* big *(page 130) before* cat.

## DOG

Bend in the index and middle fingers of both hands, almost like they're knees or maybe paws. Keep your hands side by side and move them forward and to the side.

**We used animals as symbols for our bands, clans, and of life. We used them in our stories and in our names. Animals also provided us with warmth by way of their fur and with food, especially the buffalo.**

# EARTH

OPPOSITE: The author signing the word *mountains* (page 73)

## EARTH

## RIVER

The signs for *snake* (page 27) and *river* are similar, but the starting position differs. For *snake*, you begin by pointing diagonally away from the body and drawing your finger toward you; for *river*, you begin directly to the left and trace along the horizon. The movements differ as well. For *river*, use a more gentle, flowing motion, tracing the bends in the river.

## HILL

With your right index finger, trace the shape of a hill, making an undulating motion up and down and right to left.

## MOUNTAINS

Using the same finger positioning described in *bear* (page 66), pull your fingers back and alternate moving your hands up and down vertically, almost like you're climbing, while turning your body slightly from side to side.

## TREE

To get specific about what type of tree you're talking about, you can draw its shape in the air with your fingers. For example, if you're talking about a pine tree, start with your index fingers at the top of the tree and zigzag in and out down to the base, in the shape of a Christmas tree.

## GRASS

## DIRT

Mime picking up a pinch of dirt with your right hand.



## GROUND

## DIG

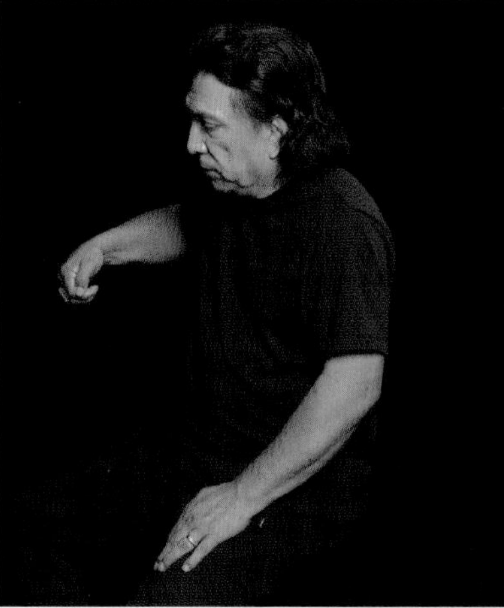

With your palm facing down and your hand cupped, reach your hand forward and pull back, like you're going in for a scoop.

*You would use this same motion for digging in the dirt as you would, say, digging through a pile of clothes.*

## PLANT

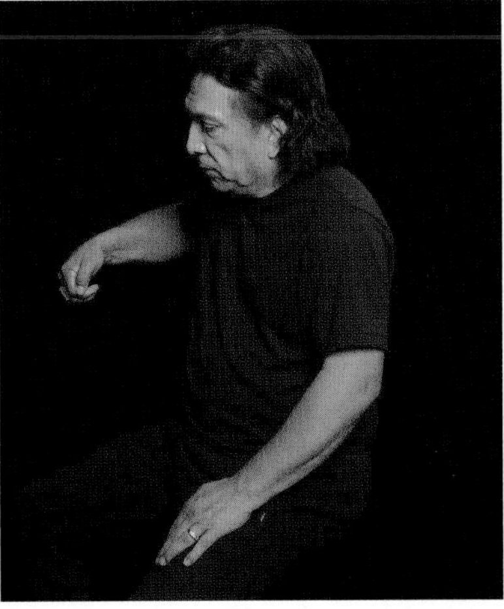

ABOVE: After signing the word for *dig*, pinch your index finger and thumb together, then separate them, as if dropping a seed into the earth.

## CROP

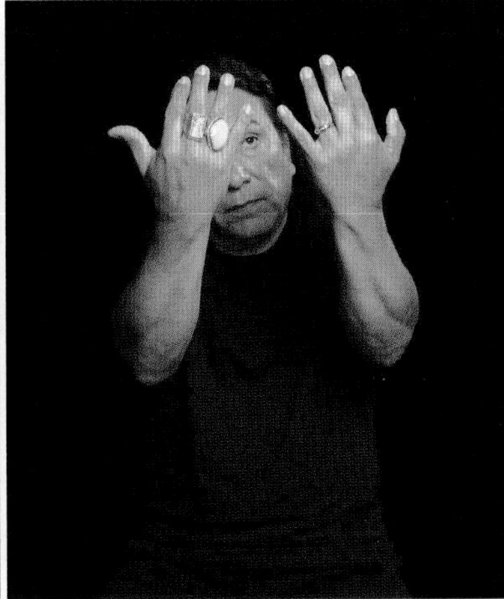

LEFT: The second half of the sign is similar to *grass* (page 73) but the gesture is larger.

## ROPE

Your right hand should be in a fist with your index finger and thumb pointing out. Then, pull back. Close the index finger and thumb into your fist as you do so.

# FAMILY

OPPOSITE: The author signing the word *baby* (page 81)

## MAN

## WOMAN

Make a gesture showing long hair on the right side of your head.

## FATHER

Place your right hand over the right side of your chest.

---

*Note the difference in hand placement for* father *and* mother. *With* mother, *the right hand goes over the left side of your chest.*

## MOTHER

I often add a small tilt of my head when I put my hand to my heart in *mother* to show that she's dear to me. While American Sign Language uses facial expressions to help underscore the meaning of signs, Hand Talk generally doesn't. In my research, I've watched other hand talkers and noticed they have no expressions on their face as they talk. But our old Native storytellers would get very animated when they told stories—really get into it. So, I think when we use Hand Talk there should still be some kind of mood. So something like a small head tilt when I put my hand to my chest with *mother* helps convey the sense of someone close to my heart.

## CHILD/CHILDREN

When signing about children, hand talkers will often point to their side, too, because children stand by their parents.

## SON

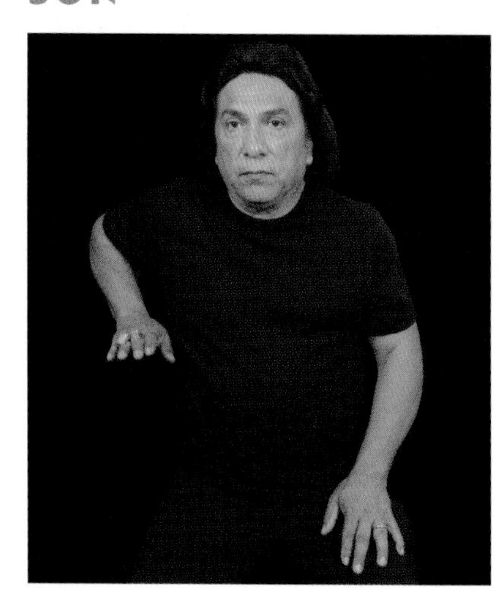

When indicating which son or daughter, you can use your right hand to show their stature to differentiate them after signing their gender. For example, a teenage son would be signed by showing a stature near your shoulder, whereas your two-year-old daughter would be indicated by a stature by your knees.

## DAUGHTER

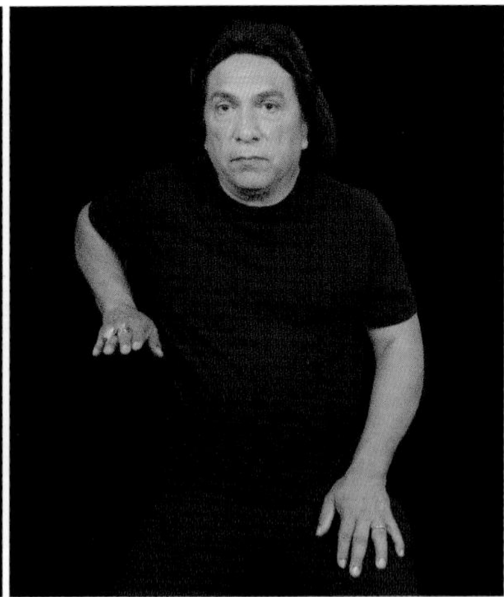

## BROTHER

Sign *man* (page 78), then turn your right index and middle fingers toward you. Touch your lips, then take your fingers away from the mouth.

## SISTER

Sign *woman* (page 78), then follow the same closing steps as *brother*. Turn your right index and middle fingers toward you, touch your lips, then take away the fingers.

## BABY

Position your left hand up and your right hand below, as if cradling a baby.

## WIFE

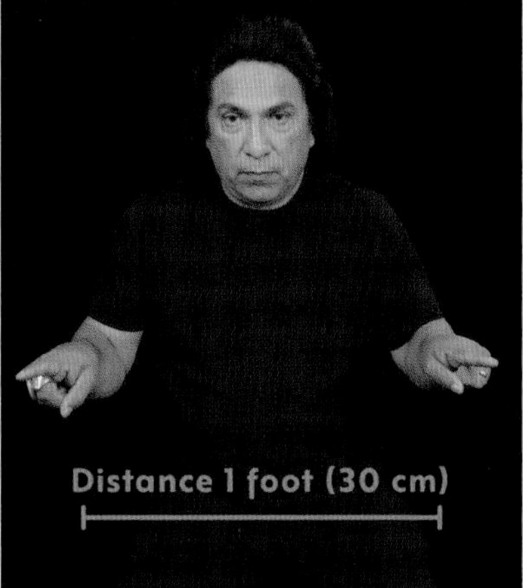

## HUSBAND

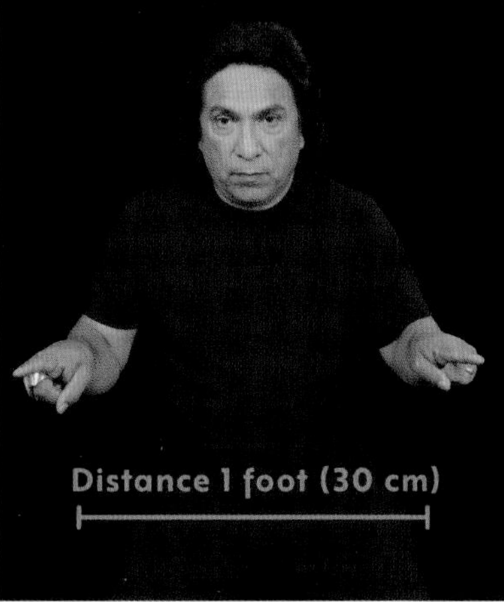

## GRANDMOTHER

The signs for *grandmother* and *grandfather* begin with holding your two fists atop each other, as if you're holding a walking stick.

## GRANDFATHER

My great-grandfather hadn't been able to hear since he was twelve years old, so he made noises rather than words. They say he was very animated in his sign language, so much so that it was understood by even non-Natives. He had no problem communicating. He was even a leader on the council; they learned Hand Talk from him.

## FRIEND

## PEOPLE

With both of your index fingers pointing up, alternate moving them slightly up and down.

## MARRY

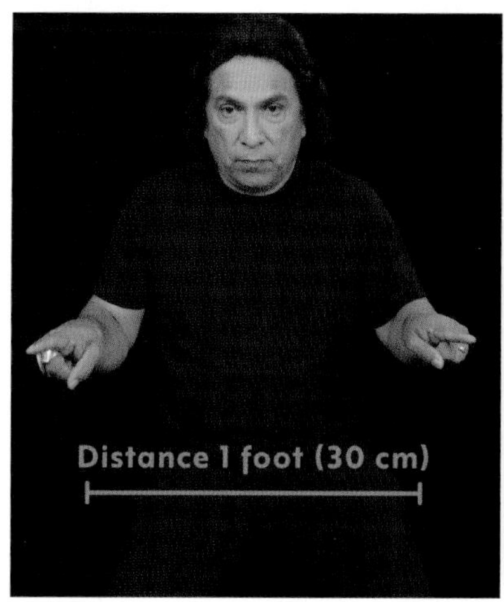

## HOME

This sign can indicate any building if you add descriptors; for example, you can sign *big* (page 130) before this sign to indicate a big building.

## I LIVE HERE

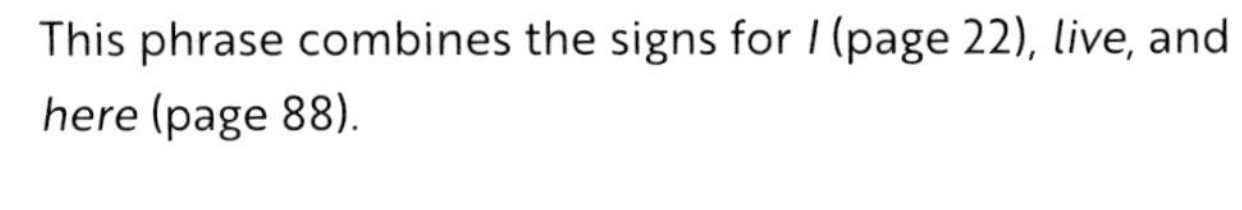
This phrase combines the signs for *I* (page 22), *live*, and *here* (page 88).

## MOVING

Place your fingers into a triangle shape (see *home* on page 83), then move your fingers from the centerline to the right.

## KEEP CLOSE

Begin with your right hand closed into a fist moving outward from the centerline, then bring the right fist to your chest.

## WORK

Place your right fist above your left, then hammer the right fist down into the left.

## MAKE

As your open palms face each other at the centerline a few inches apart, tilt the hands back and forth in sync.

---

*In some tribes, the signs for* work *and* make *are the same.*

## BUY

Place your left palm, thumb up, at the centerline. Point your right finger up, then come down to tap the side of the left index finger.

# DIRECTIONS

OPPOSITE: The author and his daughter, Heaven, signing the word *below* (page 91)

## RIGHT

## LEFT

How would we apply these signs? If someone were asking us for directions on a hike, we would turn to look at or toward the right direction and sign these words.

## AMONG

With the left palm open, weave your right index finger between the extended fingers of the left hand.

## HERE

You're not just pointing down; you need to make a downward motion at the same time.

## RIGHT HERE

Your right index finger starts chest high at the centerline, then points down to touch your left palm.

*What's the difference between* here *and* right here? *Think of it this way:* here *is more general ("I'm here at this location"), but* right here *is more specific ("I'm right here, in front of you").*

## AT

Hold your left hand up with the palm facing your right. Point to your left palm with your right index finger about a foot (30 cm) away, then bring the index finger to touch your left palm.

## IN FRONT

Begin by turning your body slightly to the left and pointing both the left and the right fingers in that direction. Position your right index finger behind the left. Then, circle your right index finger forward, where it should end up in front of the left index finger.

## BEHIND

This is very similar to *in front* (page 89), but you bring the right index finger behind the left finger instead.

---

*These signs are similar to the ones for* past (page 36) *and* future (page 37), *but the key is in the positioning. When talking about time, the fingers begin by touching and moving in a line; for* in front *and* behind, *the movement is around to the side.*

## AHEAD

## ON TOP

Hover your right hand on top of your left.

---

*Pay attention to the positioning of the hands. In* below, *the left hand hovers over the right.*

## BELOW

## AROUND

For *around*, your right finger points down and makes a circle.



## OVER

Your right hand moves over whatever object you're going over.

---

*In the photos shown here, we're indicating going over a bridge or a hill. The emphasis is the right hand going over.*

*The phrase* cross over *is performed very similarly to* over*, but the motion of the right hand is longer. What's the difference?* Cross over *is used when you're going over a longer distance—like if you were crossing over a river to get to your destination instead of a bridge or hill.*

# ACTION WORDS

OPPOSITE: The author's daughter signing the word *dance* while the author demonstrates the word

## BLESS

The palms should be open together at the centerline with the index fingers touching. Move your palms apart from each other, first in an outward direction and then slightly facing down, as if you're pressing your palms against a glass window.

## BREAK

## CLIMB

This sign looks similar to *mountain* (page 73), but the motion is more exaggerated.

## CARRY

There are two ways to express the word *carry*.

LEFT: Place your hands palms up in front of you. The arms should be bent at the elbows.

RIGHT: Place your right fist over your right shoulder with the left fist underneath, as if you are carrying a bag over your shoulder.

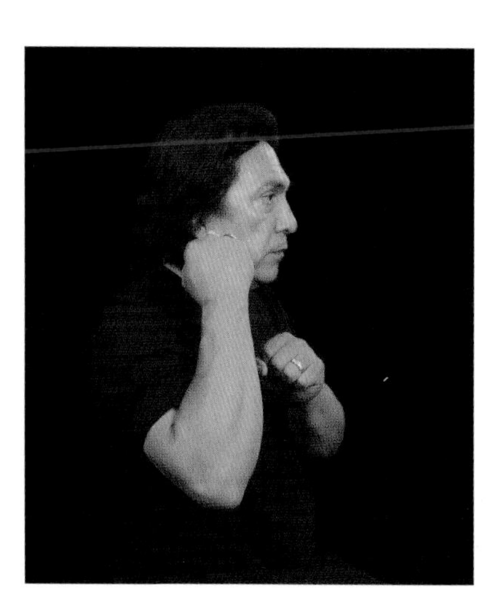

---

*Don't let your hands wander too far forward when signing* carry; *otherwise, it will look like* give.

## CRAWL

Bend your elbows with your fists at the centerline. Then, work one fist over the other, as if you are crawling.

## CRY

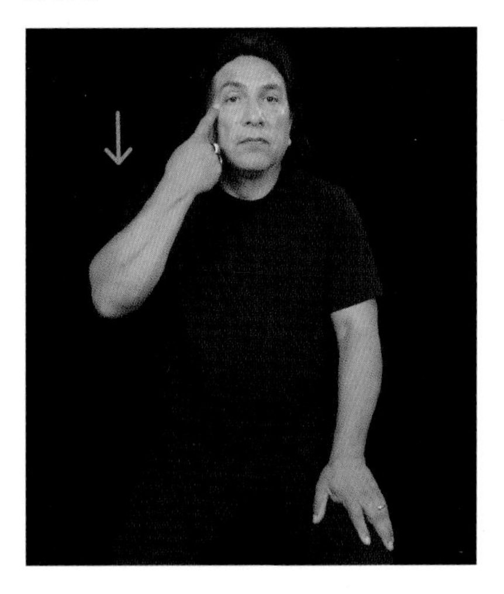

## CUT

Make a slicing motion with your right hand across your left palm.

## DRINK

It's as if you are tilting a teacup to your lips.

## GROW

With your right index finger pointing up and your palm facing the body, point upward three times.

## LAUGH

With your head tilted back, open your mouth and wave your open hands back and forth in front of the face.

## LIE

The right index and middle fingers are very close to the lips, but they don't touch.

## LISTEN

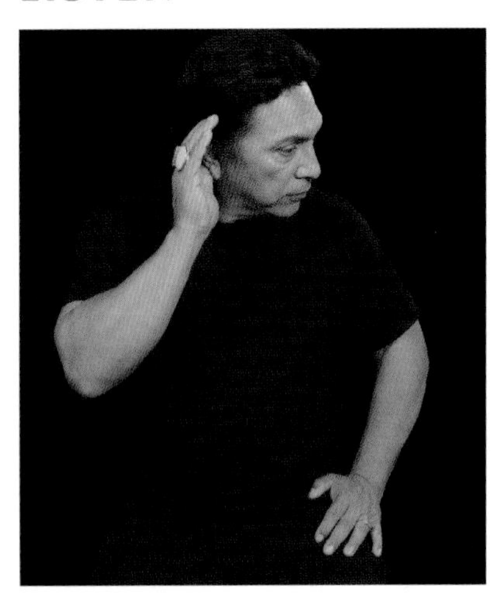

Cup your right hand to your right ear, then point in the direction of what you're listening to.

## SPEAK

As with *lie* (page 97), the index finger and thumb of your right hand are close to your mouth, but they do not need to touch it.

BELOW: Show your words "ascending" by making a twirling motion upward with your right index finger.

## PRAY

## SING

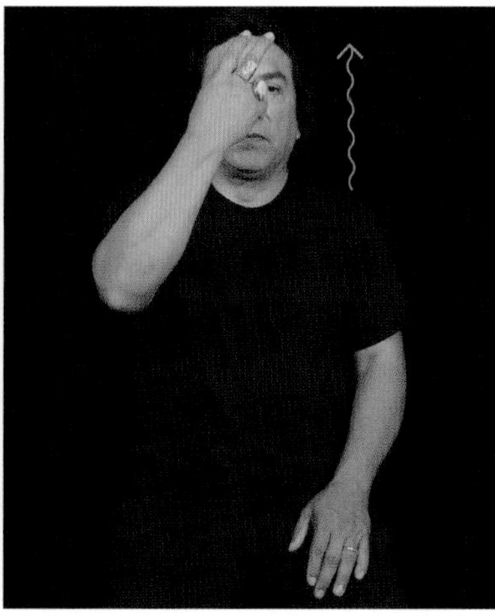

You can tilt your head back here to "show" a projecting sound.

BELOW: The word *swim* begins with the sign for *water* (page 119) and then a motion as if you're swimming the front crawl.

## SWIM

## SIT

## TRADE

Make sure the index fingers remain pointing out as you sign this word.



## WALK

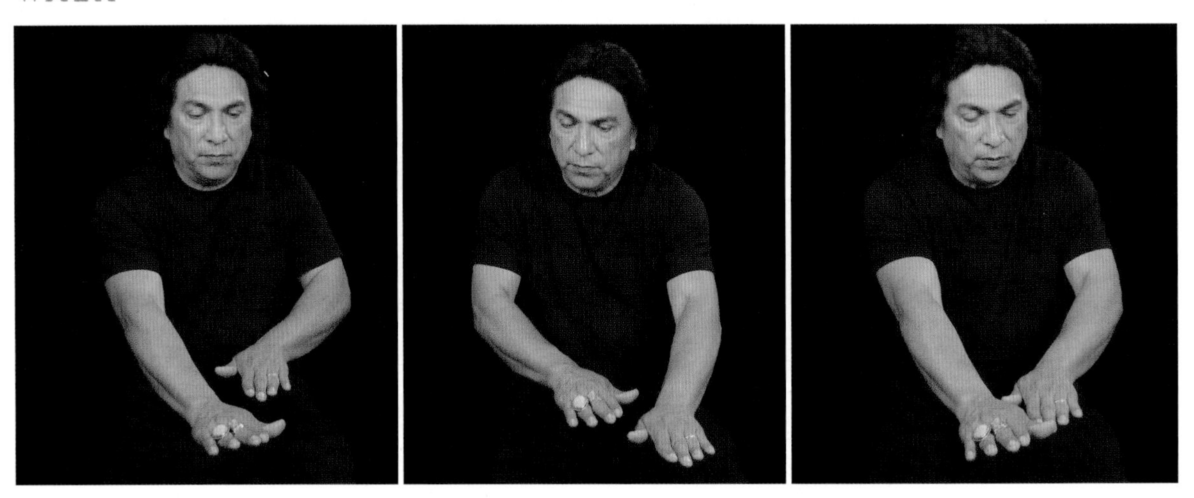

With your palms open and facing down, alternate "steps" in a walking motion.

---

*There was a time when the sign for* run *(page 24) was the same as* walk, *just moving the "feet" faster.*

## LIKE

Place your right hand over your chest, close to the centerline. This sign looks similar to *father* (page 78) at first glance, but the difference is in your hand's position relative to the centerline. Your hand is farther away from the centerline in the sign for *father*.

## AVOID

Push your right hand away from your body, then bring it back to your right side.

## OPEN

Position your palms so that they are facing outward from you. Your left thumb should rest on top of your right thumb. Then sweep your palms to the sides, in a rainbow motion.

---

*It's as if the heavens are opening.*

## CLOSE

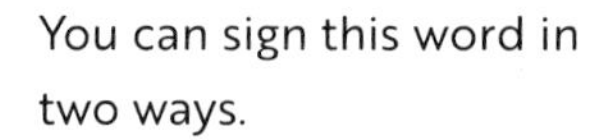

You can sign this word in two ways.

LEFT: With the heels of your hands touching each other, close the palms together.

BELOW LEFT: With your palms outstretched about a foot (30 cm) apart, bring your hands together, crossing your right thumb over your left.

*The first sign can also be used for closing a book. The second sign is more like closing something that was open (for example, a set of curtains).*

## GIVE

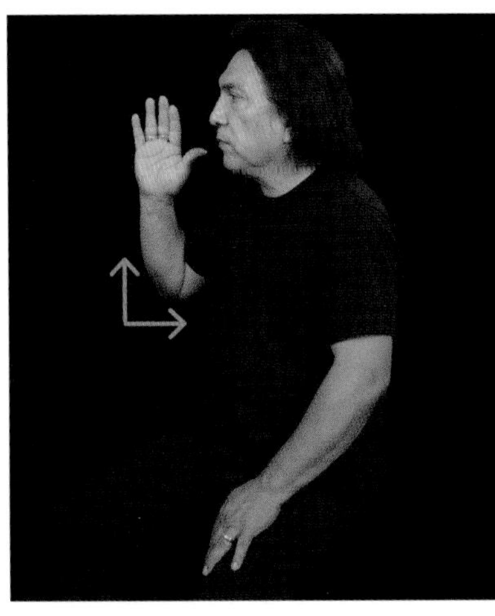

Position your right arm at a 90-degree angle in front of the body. Then, lower your right hand toward your audience, with the hand open and your palm facing you.

*There are a few different signs for* give *depending on what kind of giving you're doing. To give someone blankets or clothes, extend both hands, palms up, toward your audience—as if presenting them with something. If someone in power is distributing something, move your right open palm from your chest outward in a sweeping gesture.*

## KEEP

With your right hand outstretched, make a gripping motion, then pull the hand close to your chest. Then, place the left hand over the right fist at your chest.

## TAKE

Extend your arm, with the right index finger facing away from you at first. Then turn the index finger toward you as you draw your arm toward you and fold your finger into a fist. The sign ends with your closed fist at your chest.

## STEAL

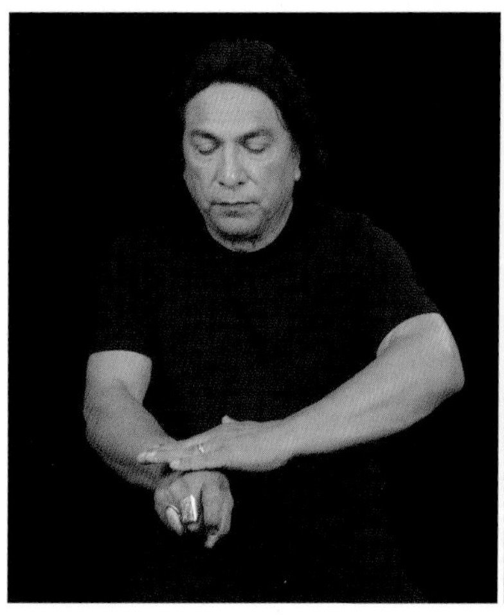

*Steal* is similar to *take*, but the action is performed under the left hand and the fist does not have to end at chest level.

*If you're stealing, you're covering up what you're doing.*

## PUSH

Raise two clenched fists, then nudge them forward.

## PULL

## SEPARATE

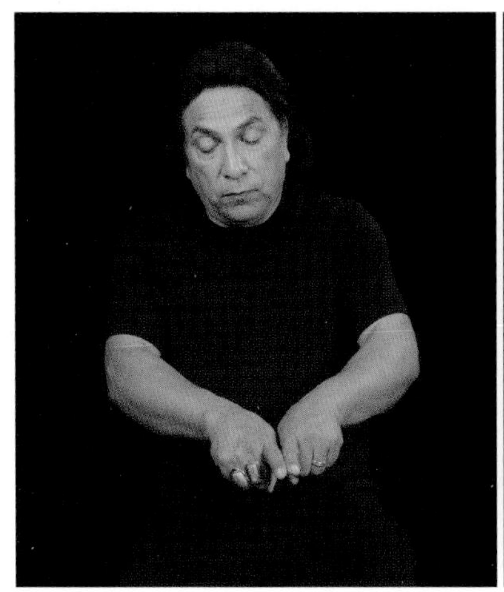

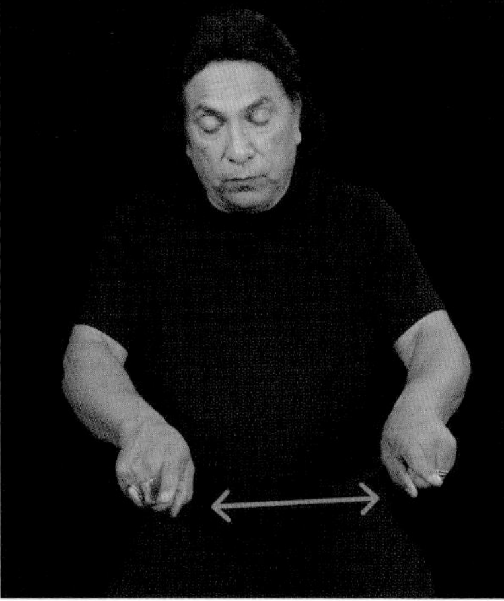

Begin with the index fingers of both hands touching, then slowly move them apart.

---

*Other signs that mean* separate *are pulling/ripping something apart with your hands.*

## HEAR

## HEARING

## SEE

Make sure that your fingers are held up at eye level.

## LOOK/LOOKING

Note that this is very similar to *see*, except that your eyes follow the direction of your fingers.

## THINK

Place your right finger to the right side of your forehead and tap it gently.

## ABUSE

## YELL

To sign *yell*, tilt your head back. The tilted head means your voice is carrying farther, up and out.

## FIGHT

Shimmy your fists back and forth for this sign, like a boxer landing quick punches.

## HIT

Drive the right fist into your open left palm.

## HURT (PHYSICAL)

Indicate a stabbing motion in the ribs with your right index, middle, and ring fingers.

## OFFEND

## SLEEP

## STAY

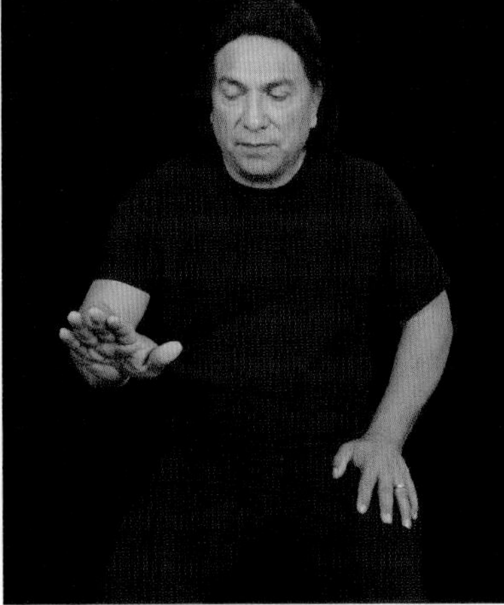

Sign *here* (page 88), then open your right palm toward your audience. The right palm should be angled downward. As you angle the hand downward, the hand moves forward slightly at the same time.

## DIE

To indicate *burial*, lower your palm farther down from *die*.

# HEALTH

OPPOSITE: The author signing the word *medicine* (page 112) while his daughter signs the word *man* (page 78); together, these two words become *doctor* (page 113)

## MEDICINE

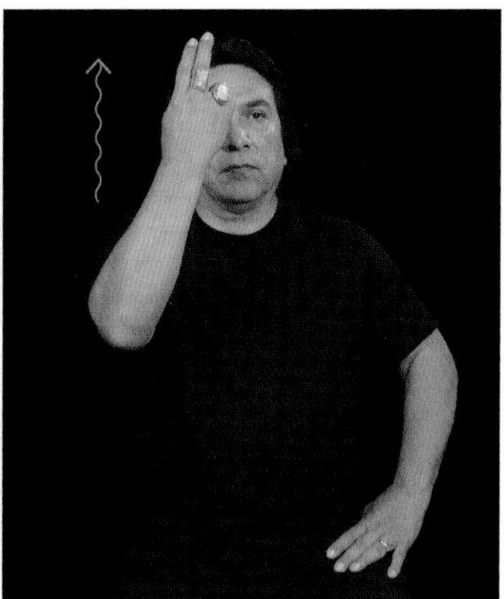

Raise the index and middle fingers of your right hand, with the inside of the fingers facing your body. Then, move the fingers upward in a swirling motion.

*The signs for* medicine *and* doctor *can vary by tribe, because there's so much diversity in cultures. I use the ones we use here in Oklahoma.*

## DOCTOR

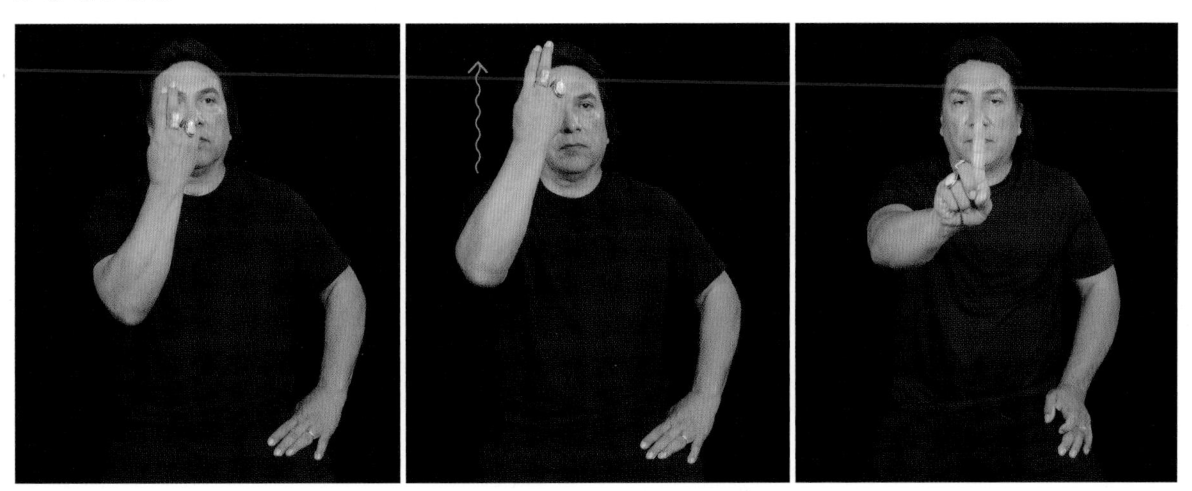

This word combines the signs for *medicine* (page 112) and *man* (page 78).

---

*The sign for* doctor *depends on who we're talking about. If we're talking about a Native doctor, we'd touch the skin, meaning* Native. *For Caucasians, we sign the word for* non-Native, *which is running the right finger over the brow, meaning "heavy brow."*

*The word for* doctor *also refers to a traditional medicine man. To express that you need to go to the* doctor, *combine the words for* hurt *(page 108),* doctor, *and* go *(page 24). Hand Talk is direct. Think of the most straightforward way to say what's on your mind, and you'll be in the right mindset.*

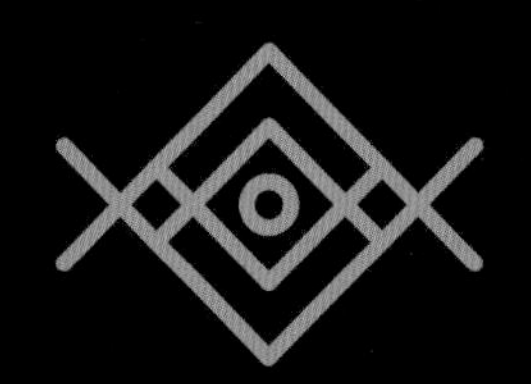

# TIME TO EAT

OPPOSITE: The author's daughter signing the word *water* (page 119); the author is signing the word *eat* (page 117)

## BREAD

Move your right and left hands over and below each other, as if shaping a piece of dough.

## MEAT

With your left palm facing up at the centerline, press your right palm down on top of your left.

## THIN

Holding the right hand vertically, pinch your palm and the back of your right hand with your left index finger and thumb.

## THICK

Holding the right arm vertically, pinch your right wrist with the index finger and thumb of your left hand, almost where you'd take your pulse.

## EAT

Bring the four fingers of your closed right hand to your lips.

## BREAKFAST

This word combines the signs for *morning* (page 46) and *eat*.

## LUNCH

This word combines the signs for *noon* (page 46) and *eat* (page 117).

## DINNER

This word combines the signs for *evening* (page 47) and *eat* (page 117).

## CHEW

Open and close the fingers and thumb of your right hand, as if mimicking a chewing motion.

## HUNGRY

Place your right arm, palm side up, across your chest.

## FULL

## WATER

You would use this sign more in the context of drinking water.

## TASTE

The difference between *taste* and *eat* (page 117) is that *taste* is only bringing your index and middle fingers up to the lips in a light motion. *Eat* uses the four fingers of the right hand.

**Whether you want bread, water, or coffee, make a hand sign for *hungry* or *eat*. Maybe the coffee is hot! Or the water is cold. Food is good. When you are full, you can say so. Combine whatever signs you need to express what you're thinking or feeling.**

## I/ ME HUNGRY LIKE EAT

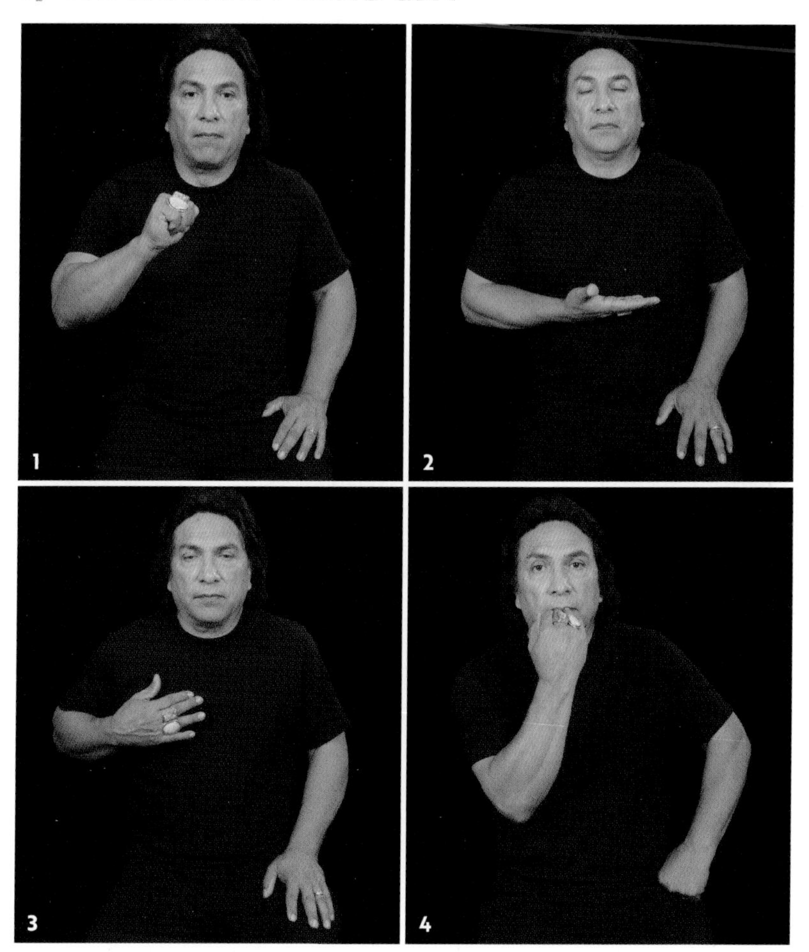


This phrase combines the words for *I/Me* (page 22), *hungry* (page 119), *like* (page 101), and *eat* (page 117). In English, this phrase would translate to "I would like to eat."

# MODERN LIFE

OPPOSITE: The author's daughter signing the word *cell phone* (page 126); the author is signing the word *computer* (page 127)

## CAR

It's as if you are gripping a steering wheel at 9 and 3.



## SHOP

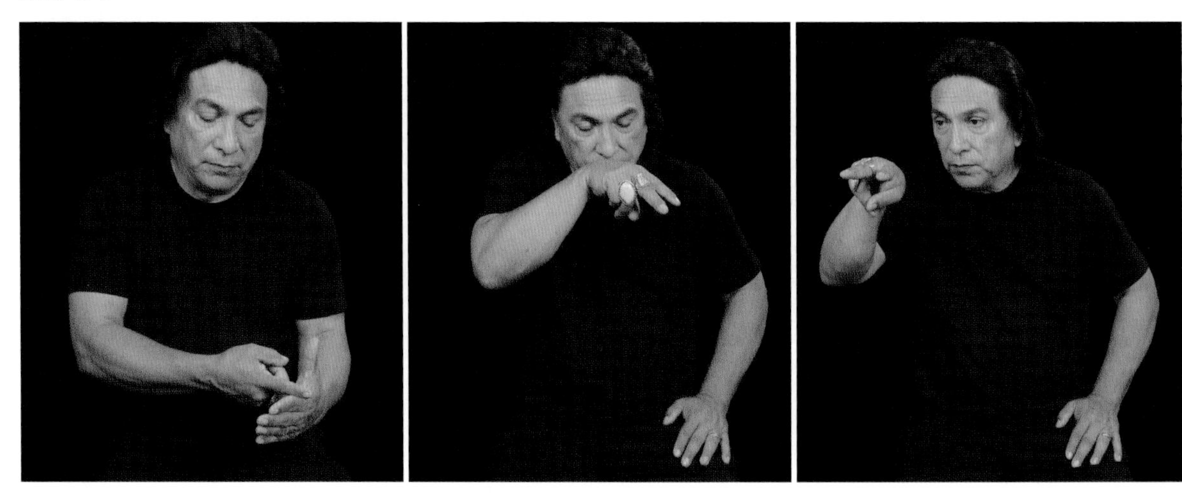

This word combines the signs for *buy* (page 85) and *looking* (page 106).

## BOOK

## REMOTE CONTROL

Extend your right hand, as if it is holding a remote control.

---

*My home life is modern. We use a remote control for a big screen TV. To describe what you watch on TV, you could sign the words for* look *(page 106),* see *(page 106), or* hear *(page 105)—as simple as that. Then with your right hand you could make a motion as if you are using a remote control to point toward the TV.*

## KEY

It's as if your right fist is holding a key and turning it to open a door.

## CREDIT CARD

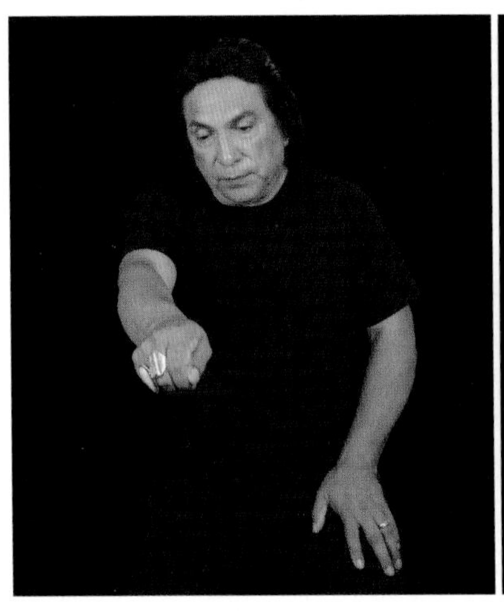

Swipe your closed right hand in front of you, as if swiping a credit card through a reader.

*Without the chip!*

## CELL PHONE

Extend your right thumb and pinky and hold them up by your ear.

*If you direct this toward a friend of yours, you could express the idea of "I'll call you."*

## MIRROR

We use a mirror to paint our faces and braid our hair. Dancers would use a mirror board for their dance routines. Our scouts and warriors once used mirrors like smoke signals. Mirrors reflect the sun's light.

## COMPUTER

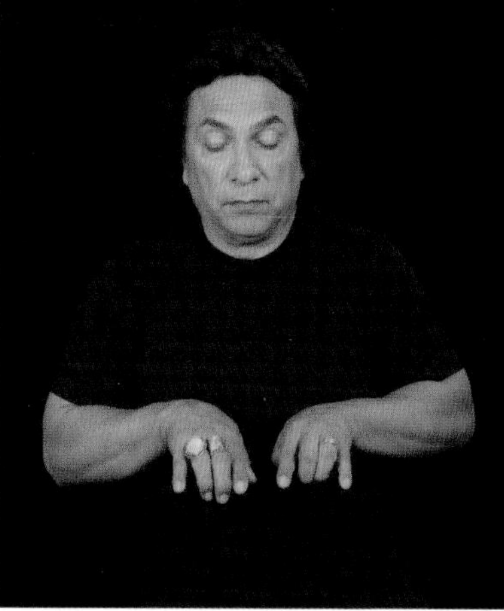

Press your palms together with the backs of your hands facing the audience. Open them as if they are the top and bottom of a laptop, respectively, then mimic typing.

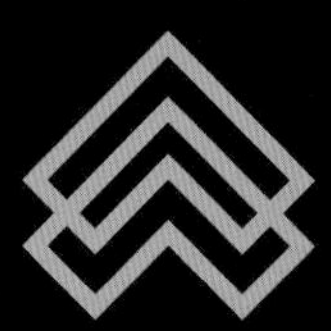

# DESCRIPTIONS

OPPOSITE: The author's daughter signing the word *deaf* (page 132); the author is signing the word *hearing* (page 105)

## POOR

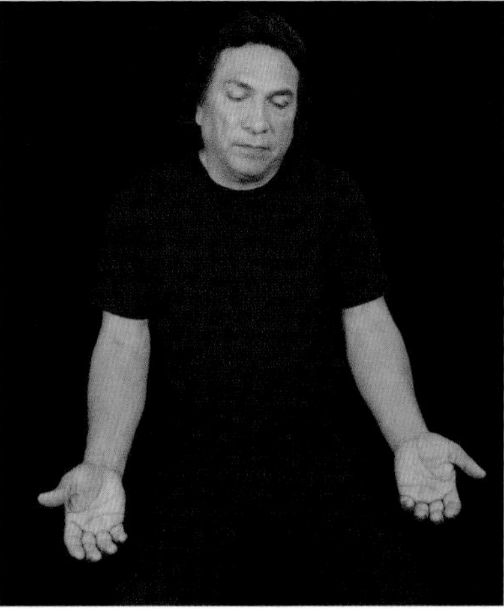

Place your hands at around waist level, then drop them lower to your side.

*More than just being related to prosperity, the word* poor *means "I have nothing." A lot of times when the word* poor *was used, it meant a humble way of looking at themselves—being low rather than just saying "I don't have money to buy things." So you can also use this sign to indicate "poor" in a figurative sense, like you're feeling poorly.*

## BIG

Make sure you use open hands when signing *big* to avoid confusion with *day* (page 47), which uses a similar motion.

## SMALL

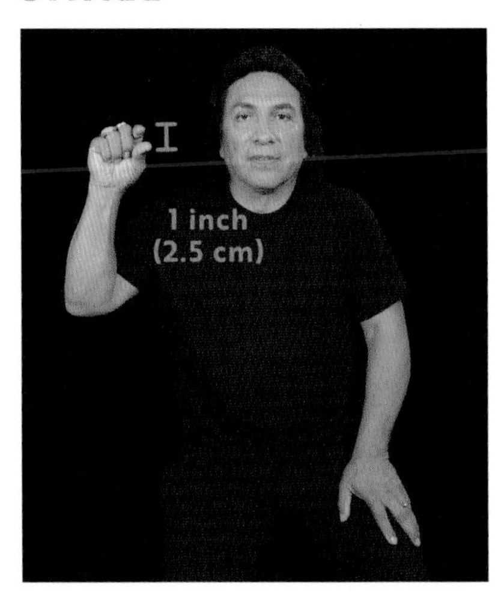


## HOLY

This could be used in reference to a ritual, but also an attitude.

## GOOD

## BAD

In this sign, your hand springs open, as if you're dropping something you don't want.

## DEAF

## STRONG

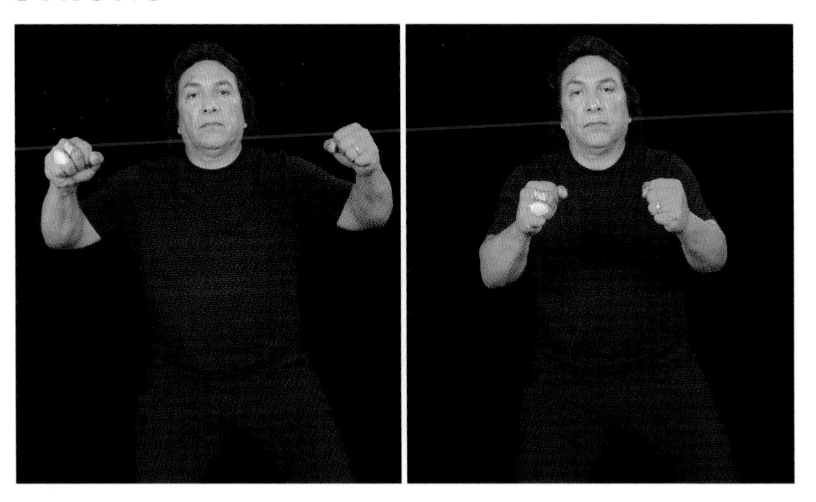

The motion for *strong* isn't so much a punch or a jolt, but a firm force.

## ALIVE

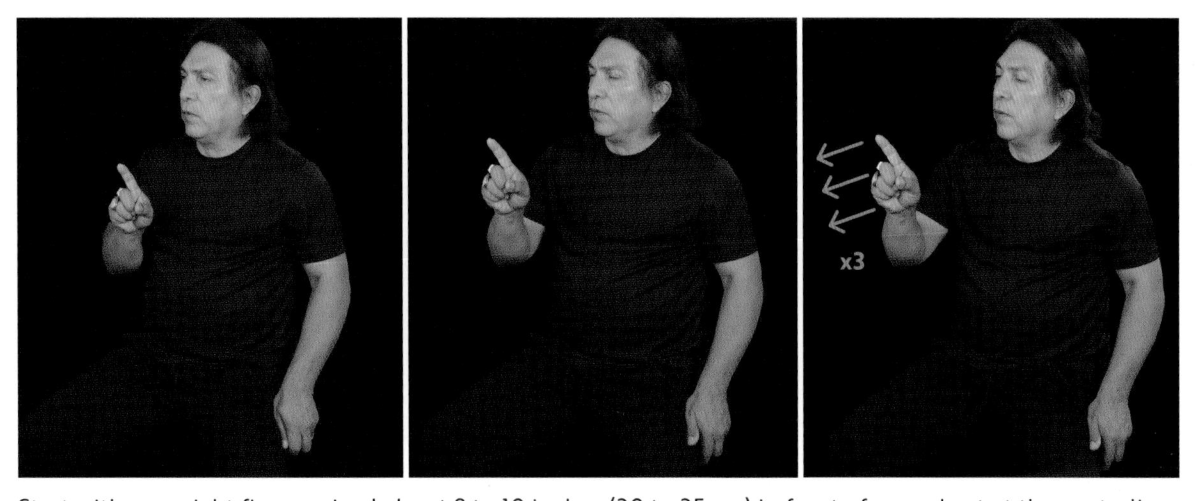


Start with your right finger raised about 8 to 10 inches (20 to 25 cm) in front of your chest at the centerline. Then, drop the right finger about 1 inch (2.5 cm) downward. Use your wrist to make three zigzag "dips" with your finger.

---

*In* alive, *your finger should make three dips in front of your body. This sign is meant to convey "you're still here, and you're walking."*

## BEAUTIFUL

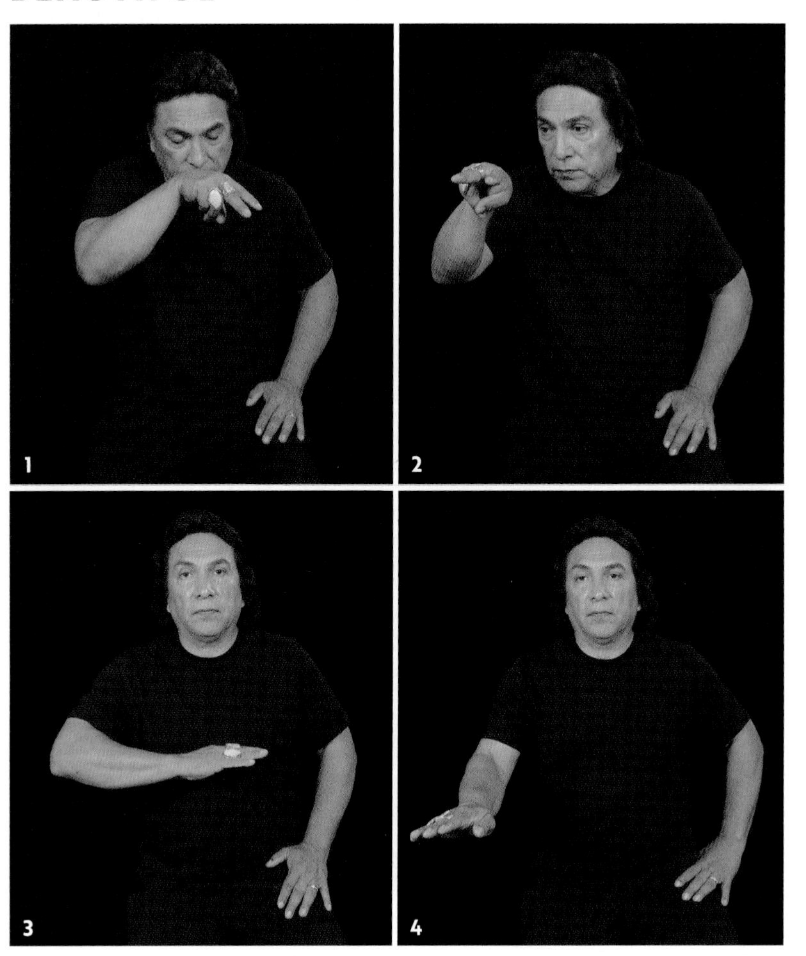

*Beautiful* uses the sign for *look* (page 106), which is very similar to *see* (page 106). In *see* your right index and middle fingers point out like eyeballs. In *look*, you move your fingers around, like eyes looking every which way.

## BITTER

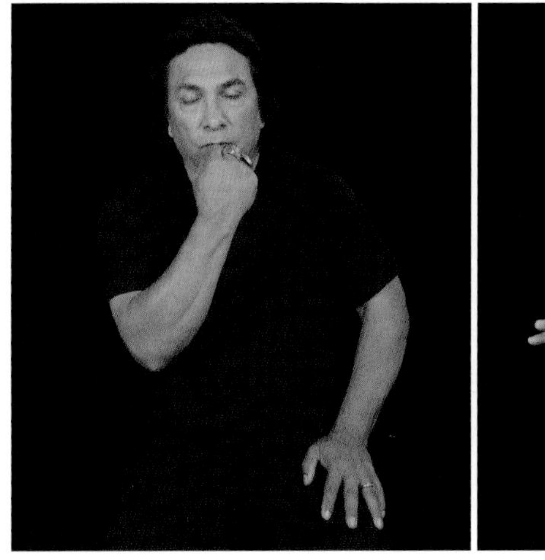

Sign the word *taste* (page 120), then move your hand out.

---

*You can pull your head back slightly here, to indicate pulling back from a bitter taste, or show an unpleasant expression on your face.*

## SWEET

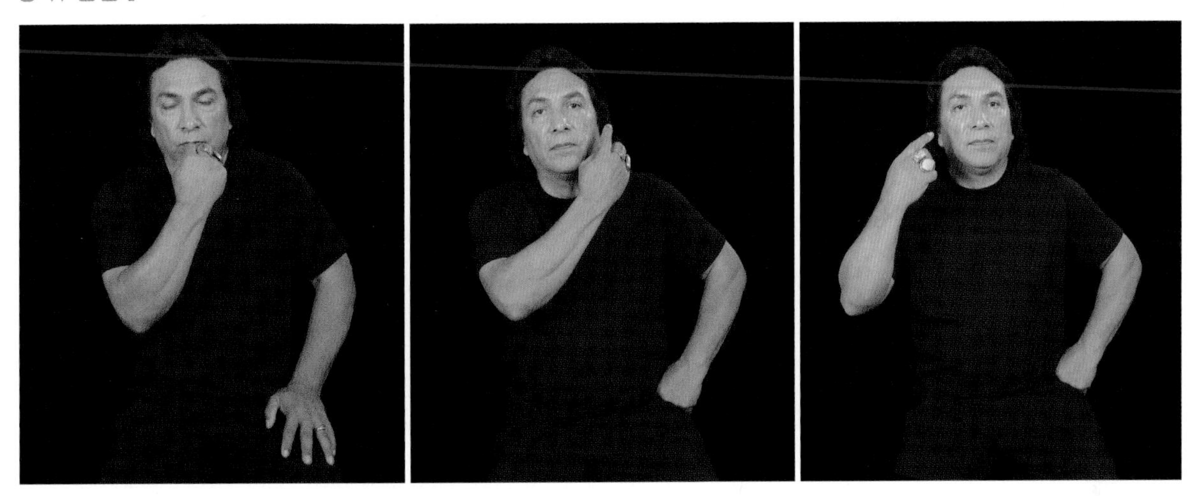

The sign for *sweet* is similar to *bitter* (page 134), but in *sweet* you use three fingers and hold the sign at your lips for a moment because it tastes good.

## OPPOSITE

The right and left index fingers should be about shoulder width apart.

# EMOTIONS

OPPOSITE: The author's daughter signing the word *love* (page 138); the author is showing another way to sign the word *sad* (page 139)

## LOVE

If you're saying "I love that" in a meaning that's more akin to *like* (page 101), you can make this sign quickly. But if you want to indicate a deeper love, you can hold the sign a beat longer or emphasize the sign with a face to show how meaningful something or someone is to you.

## HEARTACHE

For this sign, you need to jab your heart to indicate the pain. Jabbing just once means heartache, while jabbing three times emphasizes the hurt you are feeling.

## ANGRY

## SAD

Place your right fist over your heart. Tap your chest three times.

## HAPPY

Contrast this sign with *sad*.

## ANXIOUS

With your fists at chest level, pull them in opposite directions across your chest.

## DISGUST

It almost looks like I'm pointing down, but this sign is actually the one for *heart* that drops. It's showing the condition of the heart.

## TIRED

Hold your hands in front with bent elbows, then point downward with your index fingers.

*Almost like going limp!*

## AFRAID

With your index fingers pointing down and the rest of your fingers folded under, pull yourself back, as if you're afraid of something.

# QUESTIONS

OPPOSITE: The author's daughter asking *here?*; the author is asking *what?* (page 144)

**To signal that the signs that follow form a question, turn your right hand back and forth—palm up and palm down. The question indicator sign also expresses the idea of "*What?*" as there is no specific sign for that word.**

## WHAT?

The sign for *what?* is interchangeable with the question indicator sign. Whenever you intend to ask a question, start with this question indicator sign.

---

*To sign* what? *specifically, you could form the question indicator sign and then shrug with outstretched palms. You might also sweep your hand like you're searching, then turn up your palms and shrug—like, whatever it was, it's gone.*

## HERE?

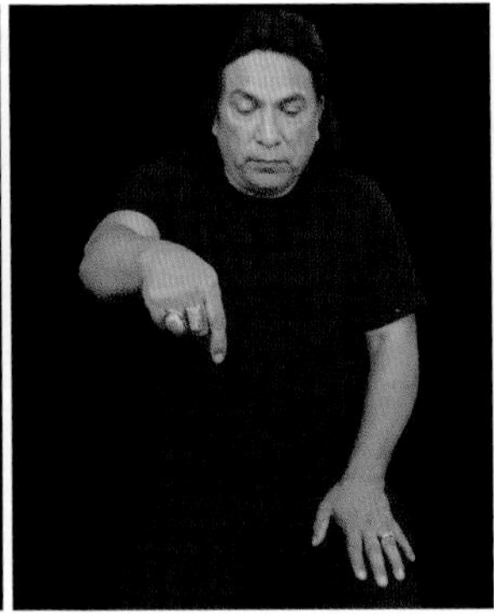

## THERE?

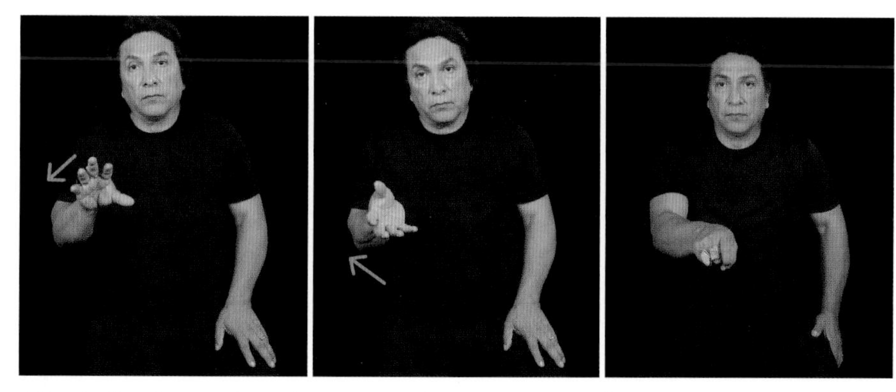

After indicating you're asking a question, point to the location you are indicating.

## THIS?

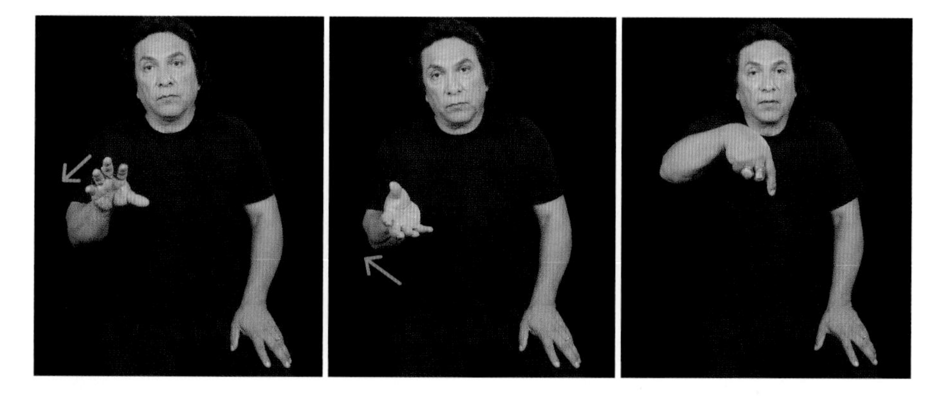

## THAT?

After indicating you're asking a question, point to the item you are indicating. This is a slightly "longer" sign than the one for *this*.

## WHY?

After indicating you're asking a question, raise your right hand and tilt it slowly to the right. As the hand begins to tilt, you can also tilt your head in the same direction to emphasize the sense of questioning.

## WHERE?

After indicating that you're asking a question, let your eyes scan the horizon with the right hand sweeping nonstop across your body, as if gesturing to possible locations.

## WHEN?

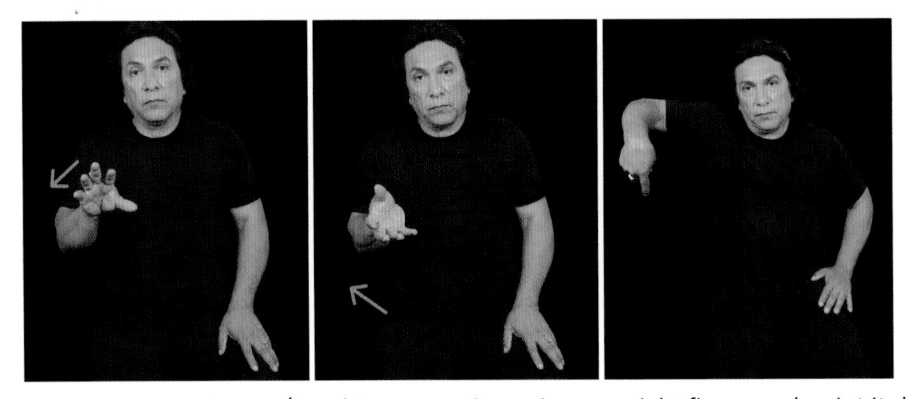

After indicating that you're asking a question, raise your right finger and point it down.

## WHO?

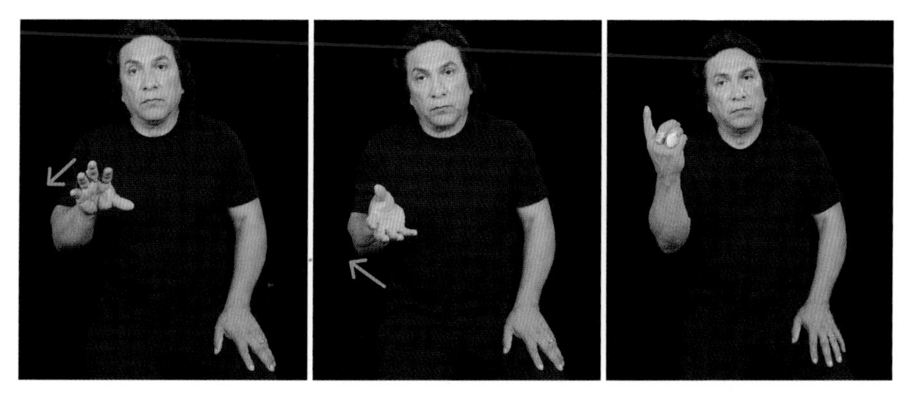

After indicating that you're asking a question, follow up by sweeping your right finger out across in front of you, as if pointing to possible people.

## WHICH?

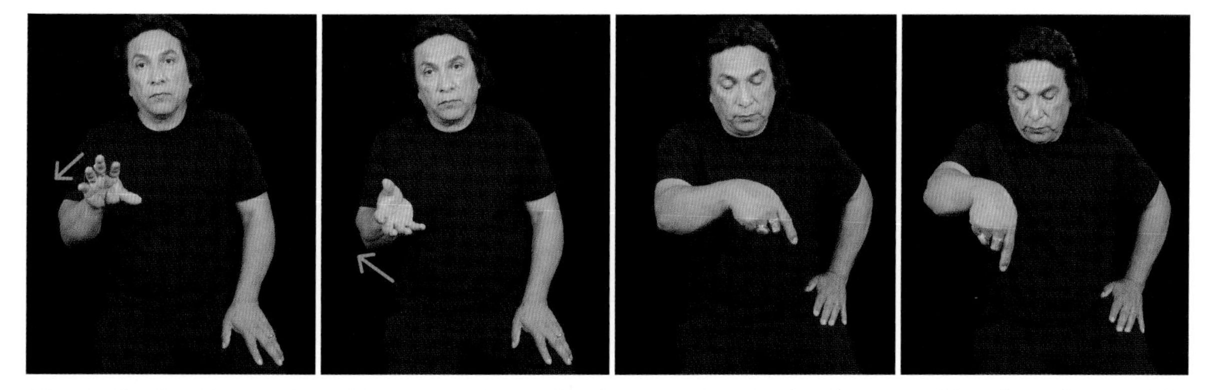

After indicating that you're asking a question, point downward a couple of times, as if you're trying to pick out *which*ever you're looking for.

# BASIC PHRASES

OPPOSITE: The author and his daughter signing the word *hello* (page 150)

## HELLO

Make sure the hand isn't out in front of you. That means *stop* if straight forward, or *attention* (page 155), if waved up near the face.

## I/ME NAME . . .

This phrase combines the signs: *I/Me* (page 22) and *name*. To sign the word *name*, place your right index finger to your lips, then move it up and to the right, away from them. In English, this phrase would translate to "My name is . . ."

## WHAT NAME?

Sign these words in the following order: the question indicator sign (page 144), *you* (page 22), and *name*. In English, this phrase would translate to "What's your name?"

## GOOD SEE YOU

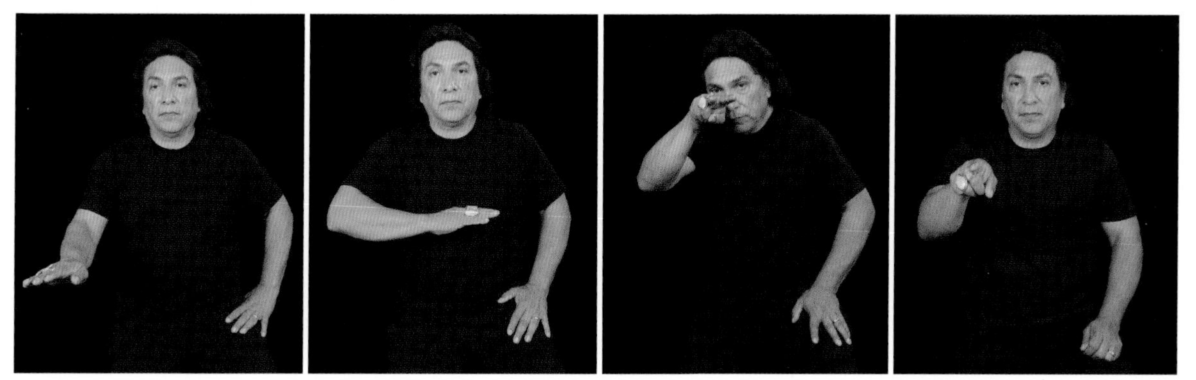

This phrase combines the signs for *good* (page 131), *see* (page 106), and *you* (page 22), and is translated into English as "It was good to see you."

---

*In Native culture, there was never a word for* goodbye. *It was always "I'll see you again"* or *"I'll see you later."*

# COUNCIL MEETINGS

OPPOSITE: The author signing the word *people* (page 83);
his daughter is signing the word *words* (page 155).

**Council meetings are held with tribe members, and they follow protocols for the order in which they are conducted. The meetings have structure and rules, but we can bend the rules a little bit, because I know everyone has meetings, so these signs can be used for those too.**

## GREETINGS

This is almost like a handshake.

## COUNCIL

The fists start out together with the palms facing the audience, then they circle away from the body and meet again at the centerline, with your palms facing your body.

## ATTENTION

There are two ways to express the word *attention.*
LEFT: You can raise a finger and poke it upward three times.
RIGHT: You can wave an open palm slightly three times.

---

*This was a way to alert council members that you had something to say. After making this gesture, you would be called on to speak.*

## MEETINGS

## PRIVATE TALK

LEFT: Note that this is the sign for *speak* (page 98), but behind the left hand.

---

*Similar to the sign for steal (page 104), you're covering up what you're doing.*

## WORDS

## TALK

Place your closed right fist by your mouth. Then, open your index finger and thumb.

## CONVERSATION

Your hands should be raised and facing each other, with the index finger and thumb of both hands pinched. Then, open the index finger and thumb of the right hand. Close the space. Then repeat the motion with your left hand, as if your hands are "talking" to each other.

## DISCUSSION

This word combines the signs for *talk* and *conversation*.

## CHIEF

With your right finger raised, sweep the finger from the crown to the back of the head, miming the feather bonnet that chiefs wear.

## YES

Point your right index finger up, with the inside of your finger facing the audience. Then, point the index finger down.

## NO

With the back of your right hand facing the audience, move the hand forward, toward your body.

## ORDER

Your right fist is placed before your left, with the index fingers on each hand raised upward. Then move your hands about 3 inches (8 cm) forward.

---

*As in working together.*

## BIG CIRCLE

Similar to *circle* (page 27), draw the circle away from and toward the body. The difference is that the circle drawn in *big circle* is larger.

## I KNOW

To sign the word *know*, move your right hand outward slightly, with the back of your right palm facing the audience.

## I DON'T KNOW

To express that you don't know something, when signing *know*, move the hand out away from your body even farther, about twice the distance than you would use with *know*.

## SPEAK FROM THE HEART

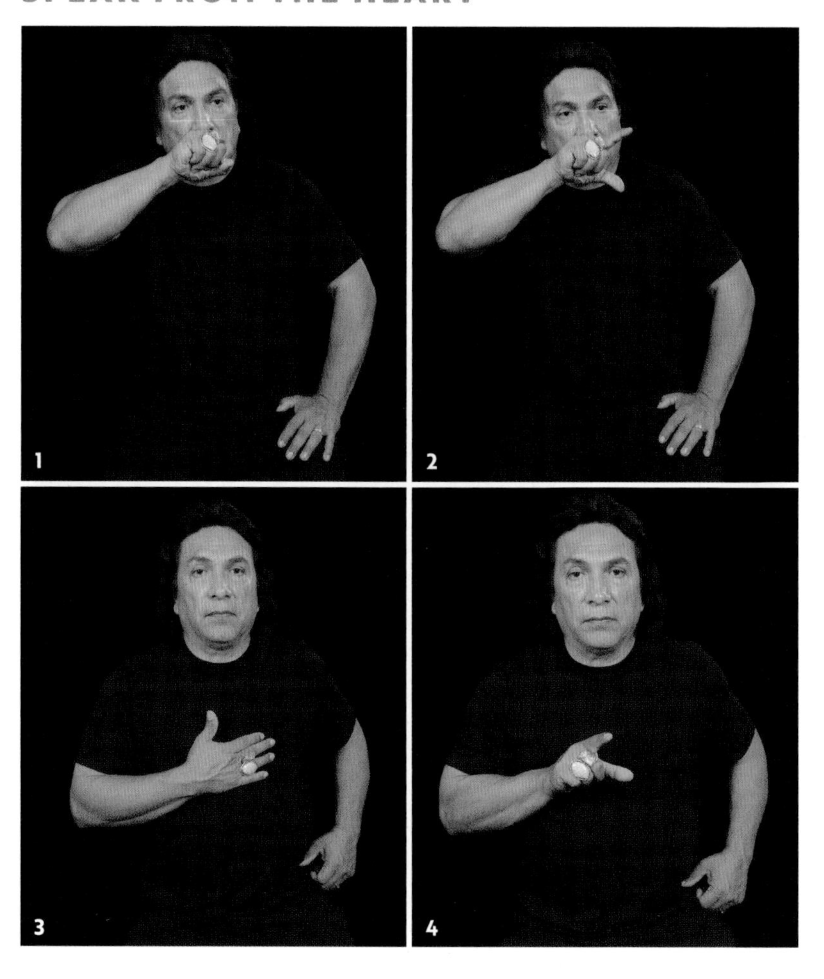

In order to say *speak from the heart*, first sign the word for *speak* (page 98). Then, lightly press your right hand over your chest, around where your heart is. After, sign the second part of the word *speak*, where you open the right index finger and thumb, but this time perform the motion by your chest. Lightly flick open the right index finger and thumb, as if you're flicking away a drop of water.

## GOOD MEET YOU

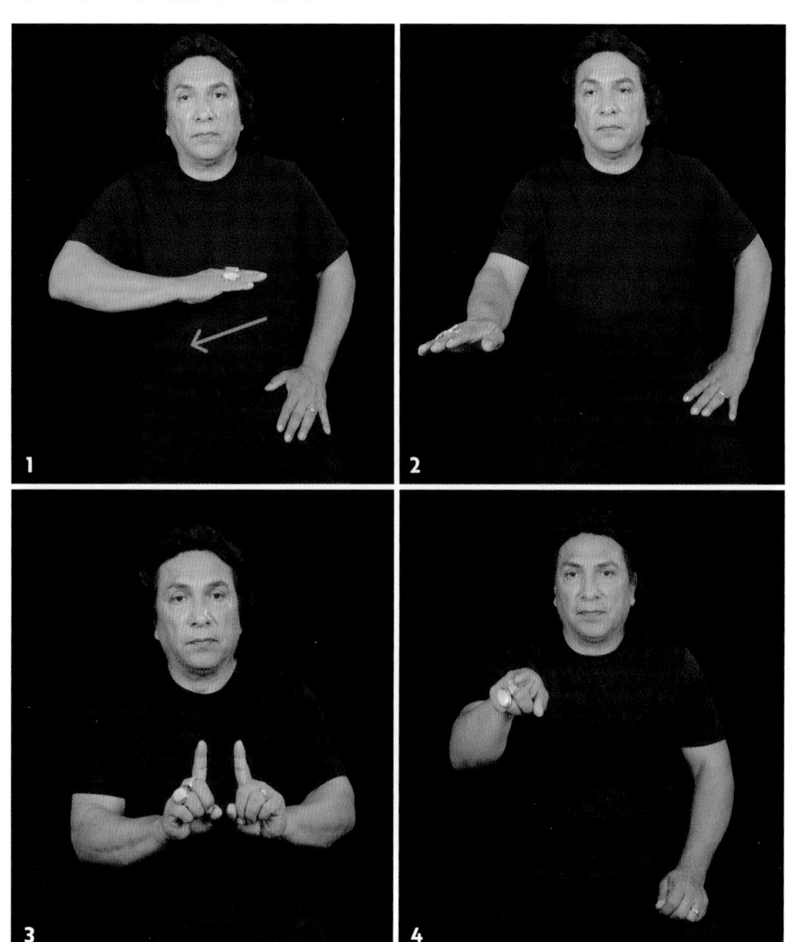


This phrase combines the signs for *good* (page 131), *meet*, and *you* (page 22).

---

*In English, this phrase would translate to "It's good to meet you."*

## DONE

Be sure to hold your hands high here. You can also punctuate this sign with an exhale.

## FINISHED

With your left arm bent up at the elbow slightly in front of you, sweep the right hand behind it, across, and down.

# REFERENCES

Chakraborty, Ranjani. "The Hidden History of 'Hand Talk.'" *Vox* video, part of their *Missing Chapter* series, 10:12. May 16, 2022. https://www.vox.com/videos/23075393/hand-talk-pisl-missing-chapter-sign-language.

Hand Talk. "1930 PISL Council." Youtube video, 34:31. March 5, 2022. https://www.youtube.com/watch?v=6JAq8lrRo5c.

Hilleary, Cecily. "Native American Hand Talkers Fight to Keep Sign Language Alive." Voice of America (VOA). April 3, 2017. https://www.voanews.com/a/native-american-hand-talker-fight-to-keep-signed-language-alive/3794333.html.

National Museum of the American Indian (NMAI), Smithsonian Institution. "Chapter 3: Boarding Schools. Struggling with Cultural Repression." Part of a Native Knowledge 360° education initiative. Accessed December 2, 2022. https://americanindian.si.edu/nk360/code-talkers/boarding-schools.

National Park Service. "Lewis & Clark National Historic Trail: American Indian Sign Language." Last updated May 27, 2021. https://www.nps.gov/articles/000/american-indian-sign-language.htm.

O'Brien, Cynthia. *National Geographic Kids Encyclopedia of American Indian History and Culture: Stories, Timelines, Maps, and More*. Washington, DC: National Geographic Kids, 2019.

Okrent, Arika. "The Signed Lingua Franca That Once Spanned North America." *Mental Floss*. May 1, 2017. https://www.mentalfloss.com/article/500499/signed-lingua-franca-once-spanned-north-america.

Perley, Logan. "Indigenous Sign Languages Once Used to Help Nations Communicate Still Being Used Today." Canadian Broadcasting Corporation (CBC). Last updated November 13, 2020. https://www.cbc.ca/radio/unreserved/breaking-barriers-unreserved-marks-indigenous-disability-awareness-month-1.5796873/indigenous-sign-languages-once-used-to-help-nations-communicate-still-being-used-today-1.5796874.

Piapot, Ntawnis. "Plains Sign Language Camp a New Spin on an Old Way of Communicating on the Prairies." CBC. Last updated December 11, 2019. https://www.cbc.ca/news/indigenous/plains-sign-language-camp-1.5283245.

Yurth, Cindy. "Several Famous Navajos Called Coyote Canyon Home." Part 22 of a series of articles entitled *Manuelito's Legacy. Navajo Times*, February 14, 2013. https://www.navajotimes.com/news/chapters/021413coy.php

# PHOTO CREDITS

Choate, J.N. Photographs taken of Hastiin To'Haali (Tom Torlino) while attending the Carlisle School. c. 1882 and 1885. Courtesy of the Beinecke Rare Book and Manuscript Library, the Richard Henry Pratt papers, Yale University.

Photograph "Grey Whirlwind, in Native Dress, Talking to Ernest Thompson Seton, Non-Native Man, Sign Language": National Anthropological Archives, Smithsonian Institution [NAA INV.00574500]

Photograph "Man in Native Dress (Son of the Star ? or Rushing Bear ?) Showing Sign Language Gesture": National Anthropological Archives, Smithsonian Institution [NAA INV.01309100]

# INDEX

## D



## E



## F

# ACKNOWLEDGMENTS

As a child, I was always fascinated by the stories and memories of my great-grandfather "Pi," as he was called. Full-blooded Osage, our family got our last name, Pahsetopah, from him. Remembered for his ability to communicate using Native American sign language, relating stories and his travels, he was a prominent and highly respected figure in his time. I have so much respect and admiration for him. I only wish that I could have talked to him and shown him that Hand Talk still lives.

I would also like to recognize and honor both my parents, Paul and Jean Pahsetopah. In their memory I dedicate this book. They gave me beautiful cultural heritage. Their teachings and ways were very instrumental, shaping my life. I've carried on everything Dad taught: his talents and gifts live on through me. Mom was a strong woman who taught us to face any challenge fearlessly. I can still hear her cheering me on.

# ABOUT THE AUTHOR

Michael Pahsetopah has been gifted with many talents and abilities. At the age of three he made his debut as a fancy feather dancer. At the age of five he showed an interest in art, taking after his father, Paul Pahsetopah, who was a renowned Native American artist. Mike credits his father for introducing him to a career path related to Native culture, as he pursued dancing and performing in Native dance troupes and became himself a well-known Native American artist, winning in art shows.

As a dancer active in American Indian theater, Mike has distinguished himself in various ways. In 1982, Mike won the Augustus McDonald World's Championship, and he used his victory as a platform to take fancy dance to new heights. He was featured as the world-class American Indian fancy dancer at Discovery Land for seventeen summer seasons and was named the Most Photographed Native American Fancy Dancer. His photos appeared in magazines, brochures, flyers, posters, ads, and on phonebook covers. Mike was also invited to France, where he danced atop the famous Eiffel Tower in Paris. In New York, he danced atop the Empire State Building. Mike has performed dances for dignitaries, leaders, companies, celebrities, and the military. He has also appeared in commercials, films, and on television. He has been credited as a language consultant on the television series *Into the Wild Frontier* and has also made appearances in such films and series as *Chasing the Wind, Gunslinger, The Last of the Mohicans,* and *Walker, Texas Ranger.*

Mike's professional title is Native American Cultural Educator/Cultural Preserver. He has been visiting public schools in the US presenting dance for forty-seven years now. As a cultural presenter he is also a storyteller, flute player, dance teacher, and specialty dancer, which includes Hoop Dance and Eagle Dance. He is the founder of his family dance troupe, internationally known as the Dancing Eagles.

Mike has been married to his wife Lisa, who is of Pawnee descent, for twenty-one years. He is the father of three children, Michael Paul, Sophia, and Heaven, and has one step-son, Chance Fields. His immediate family also includes five grandchildren, one great-grandson, and three step-grandchildren.

An enrolled member of the Muscogee Creek Nation, he is also of Yuchi descent. He is of Osage/Cherokee descent on his father's side, where he gets his sign language.

First published in 2023 by Wellfleet Press, an imprint of The Quarto Group,
142 West 36th Street, 4th Floor, New York, NY 10018, USA
T (212) 779-4972 F (212) 779-6058 www.Quarto.com



ISBN: 978-1-57715-366-5

10 9 8 7 6 5 4 3 2 1

Library of Congress Cataloging-in-Publication Data

Names: Pahsetopah, Mike, author.
Title: Talking with hands : everything you need to start signing Native American hand talk : a complete beginner's guide with over 200 words and phrases / Mike Pahsetopah.
Other titles: Everything you need to start Native American hand talk : a complete beginner's guide with over 200 words and phrases
Description: New York : Wellfleet Press, 2023. | Includes bibliographical references and index. | Summary: "Talking with Hands is a guide to learning Plains Indian Sign Language, once used widely between the Indigenous peoples of what is now called the Great Plains of North America"-- Provided by publisher.
Identifiers: LCCN 2023000248 (print) | LCCN 2023000249 (ebook) | ISBN 9781577153665 (hardcover) | ISBN 9780760382288 (ebook)
Subjects: LCSH: Indian sign language--Handbooks, manuals, etc. | Indians of North America--Great Plains--Languages--Handbooks, manuals, etc. | LCGFT: Handbooks and manuals.
Classification: LCC E98.S5 P34 2023 (print) | LCC E98.S5 (ebook) | DDC 419/.108997--dc23/eng/20230113
LC record available at https://lccn.loc.gov/2023000248
LC ebook record available at https://lccn.loc.gov/2023000249

Group Publisher: Rage Kindelsperger
Creative Director: Laura Drew
Managing Editor: Cara Donaldson
Editor: Elizabeth You
Author Photography: Gary Thomson (Cherokee)
Cover and Interior Design: Beth Middleworth

Printed in China